IS LOVE MORE POWERFUL THAN DEATH?

When her husband Bob died, suddenly
and tragically, Victoria Stevenson was
stricken with grief. But then she found
she was able to communicate with Bob
— and he with her — and she learnt
that her grief had prevented his early
attempts at communication from being
successful.

In this book, Victoria Stevenson tells
from personal experience how she
became confident that their love lives
on, and how she derives great comfort
from her conviction that death is not the
end.

Love After Death

Victoria Stevenson

Her unique story of communication beyond the grave

CORGI BOOKS
A DIVISION OF TRANSWORLD PUBLISHERS LTD

LOVE AFTER DEATH

A CORGI BOOK 0 552 11860 5

Originally published in Great Britain as
The Triumph of Love by Arlington Books Ltd.

PRINTING HISTORY

Arlington edition published 1980
Corgi edition published 1981

This book is set in 10/11 Paladium

Corgi Books are published by
Transworld Publishers Ltd.,
Century House, 61–63 Uxbridge Road,
Ealing, London, W5 5SA

Made and printed in United States of America
by Offset Paperbacks,
Dallas, Pennsylvania.

To Bob

'Many waters cannot quench love, neither can the flood drown it –
for love is as strong as death.'

Contents

	Foreword	11
	Prologue	13
One	Night	15
Two	Past Communications	21
Three	First Whispers	28
Four	Practical Help	38
Five	The Search For Proof	43
Six	Growing Closer	52
Seven	Still Growing Closer	57
Eight	Voices On Tape	63
Nine	Seeking Proof Again	69
Ten	Direct Voices	74
Eleven	Daybreak	84
Twelve	More Practical Help	91
Thirteen	Dreaming	97
Fourteen	Still Seeking Evidence	102
Fifteen	More Communications	107
Sixteen	Still More Words	115
Seventeen	Lasting Comfort	122
	Epilogue	124

Mr. David Ellis, M.A. (Cantab) who kindly offered to write the following Foreword, held the PERROTT-WARRICK STUDENTSHIP (1970-1972) from Trinity College, Cambridge to investigate the newly discovered phenomena of the Raudive Voices on tape.

Foreword

It is a pleasure and a privilege for me to write a few words of introduction to Victoria Stevenson's book.

As you will read, I first met Victoria Stevenson on 14th August 1972, and since then I have visited her many times. I have been present at some of her talks with Bob, taken part in tape-recording and table-tilting experiments and accompanied her at sittings with Mr. David Young and Mr. Leslie Flint.

Psychical research is a difficult subject. It provides no simple, cut-and-dried answers to the problems of existence; it is baffling, ambivalent, uncertain, frustrating — and challenging. Many of us believe, from faith or religious conviction, that death is but the gateway to a fuller and better life; others, perhaps of a materialist or rationalist persuasion, believe that when our bodies perish, so do we. In studying psychical research — as, indeed, in any other scientific endeavour — such beliefs must be laid aside. We must look at the evidence, the phenomena under study, not in order to prove to ourselves or to other people that what we believe is true, but to find out whether what we believe is true or not.

In fact, the evidence for some sort of personal 'Survival' is more extensive and substantial than most people unacquainted with the history and literature of psychical research might imagine, and includes some remarkable cases of apparent communication, much that suggests purpose and intelligence, and some very strange phenomena. Many have found it sufficient for their personal conviction. However, it still could not be said to amount to scientific proof, which means that it is conceivable that we may eventually be able to explain quite satisfactorily all the 'evidence' so far obtained without any reference to postmortem survival. Probably the majority of researchers today see Survival as an insoluble problem, as an issue that may never be settled. Others are trying to tackle it in an indirect way. (Strangely enough, the major reason for today's dilemma has been the success of laboratory ESP experiments, which has made possible the counter-explanation that evidential information received through mediums could be the result of telepathy between the living rather than communication with the dead.)

Meanwhile, in the absence of conclusive evidence, all we can do is to assess what evidence there is and make our own provisional judgement; as yet, belief (one way or the other) must take the place of knowledge. I can think of few more pleasant ways of assessing a little of the evidence than reading this book. Victoria Stevenson tells her own personal story simply and accurately; she does not exaggerate nor distort the truth — and she has an excellent memory. What is more, she writes with the concise, lucid and effective style of a professional journalist.

Here is the perfect handbook for the bereaved, who will understand the desolation of Bob's death, and be comforted by the evidence of his continued presence, his concern for his wife, his practical help and inspirational communications.

D.J. Ellis

Prologue

This evening I am relaxing in my pleasant sitting-room, with the sun sinking behind the trees, casting long shadows on the lawns, and I have the strong, happy feeling that Bob is sharing this with me.

The grandfather clock in the corner ticks rhythmically on, as it has during the thirty happy years of our marriage.

At last I can begin to piece together, without undue grief, the strange story of how, it seems to me, my husband has reached out to show me that death is but a thin veil dividing us by 'half a hair's breadth'.

Through our great love I feel he can still comfort and guide me. Bereft, rudderless and drifting in grief as I was, he has shown me that love is stronger than death.

I have doubted it, turned to others for guidance and confirmation that it was not just my imagination, and now at last I feel I can write down my strange, unusual experience, to comfort others who dread the finality of death.

1 Night

For me time stopped on the 2nd April, 1971, the day Bob died.

Just as in *Joshua*, 'the sun stood still in the midst of Heaven and hasted not to go down a whole day', the stars stopped in their courses and Orion's glittering belt which, in former days, I loved to see move slowly past my window, seemed permanently halted in the sky as I awaited the dawn.

Even the second hand of the electric clock seemed to pause in its sweep as my husband's heart stopped in its struggle for life.

The dazzling beauty of winter snows and the burgeoning spring flowers scattered over my garden left me indifferent, for my senses were numbed. I saw nothing, for my grief blinded me. Bob was dead and part of me had died too.

Bob and I did not marry until our early thirties. He was a scientist, dedicated to his work as Technical Director of an old-established firm of Scientific Instrument Makers and Laboratory Furnishers until 1959, when he became Technical Director of a firm specialising in chromatography and electrophoresis. In 1964 he was elected a Member of the American Association for the Advancement of Science. I was a journalist on a woman's magazine, equally dedicated to my own career.

We could not have been more different: he, precise, practical, strong-willed, and so punctual that I used to say if he had agreed to meet me at the North Pole at a certain time, he would be there no matter what hazards he had to overcome; myself, romantic, artistic, a dreamer — always running late in my own organised but rushing life (to Bob's annoyance and later forebearance, when he realised nothing could be done to change me!)

Yet we met — by sheer chance when I was on holiday with my parents, and realised on parting that we were both working in London in practically adjoining streets — and fell in love, to everyone's surprise, spending thirty happy years together.

A few months before our marriage, at the end of a charming love letter, Bob wrote, 'I am sure that what we have in store for us will be — not just a mere tolerance of the convention of what is called married life, but a love beside which that of (to use your own figures) Elizabeth and Robert Browning shall pale as the moon at the rising of the sun'. He knew I was a great admirer of Elizabeth Barrett Browning's *Sonnets from the Portuguese*.

It was a coronary that ended it all. Unexpected, swift, final. In one cruel blow, like the shattering of a crystal glass dropped by a careless hand, our lives together lay in fragments.

Bob died after a desperate, determined fight just as we had both convinced ourselves he was recovering — like the sudden switching off of the light as he slept.

He had overcome so many obstacles in his life, including the amputation of his right leg when he was twenty-one, but despite his dogged personality, his last enemy, death, he could not defeat — or so it seemed at the time.

I returned home after they told me, alone. I was like a clockwork toy — an automaton with a robot's brain. I was completely cold and detached. I could not weep.

I walked slowly up the drive and looked at the big old house which had always been so comforting and dear to me.

When we first saw it together it had been neglected, the gabled roof, tall chimneys and garden sadly falling into decay. But we took it and lovingly restored it.

Today the tall windows seemed to stare at me with dead eyes — our lovely house looked to me as bleak as I felt.

For the first time I unlocked the door myself. Bob had always swung it open for me on our homecomings together. There was no sound, except for the dragging tick of the clock and the tap of my own footsteps on the polished oak floor. I stood in the hall and looked up the curving sweep of the staircase.

How could I go on?

At the sight of Bob's wallet among his personal possessions, brought back for me from the hospital — his favourite snaps of our home tucked in it — I finally broke down. The uncontrollable tears flowed and wracked my body. I felt almost physical pain. My life was in ruins.

The world would go on — and somehow I'd have to go on too . . . but the thought kept pounding in my mind . . . I am alone now . . . alone.

For the first time in my life I felt the agony of total loneliness. Yet I remember now that even at that moment of total isolation, once I was inside, the house, strangely, seemed to welcome, even to soothe me.

Exhausted I dragged myself up the stairs to the bedroom that we had shared for so long. I lay down on the bed. Somehow, somewhere, Bob's presence seemed to linger and, to my surprise, I slept.

At first I felt I couldn't bring myself to attend the funeral. But in the end I made the supreme effort. I knew it was what Bob would have expected — that I should do the correct thing and not wallow in my grief. I doped myself with sedatives beforehand, and in the event how glad I was that I had had the courage to go.

Once when we had discussed death Bob had expressed a wish to be cremated, saying he could not bear to think of my shedding tears at his grave. I found great spiritual consolation in the beauty of the service with its message of hope. Even in the midst of my grief I felt that the real Bob was with me and that only his earthly remains, like an old cast-off cloak, lay in the purple-draped coffin resting before us. I had chosen Bob's favourite hymn — and mine:

'*Immortal, Invisible, God only wise*

17

In light inaccessible hid from our eyes . . .'
with its message of hope in the closing lines,
'. . . oh help us to see
'Tis only the splendour of light hideth Thee.'

I raised my eyes to the stained glass window in the side chapel, depicting the Risen Christ joining the two disciples on their way to Emmaus who thought him a stranger until, 'he broke bread with them' and revealed himself as their beloved Master, 'when he vanished from their sight.'

Our Vicar had known Bob as a scientist and a questing Christian. (So seriously had Bob taken the matter of life and death that I discovered after his death a file marked *Reason v Faith*, filled with his own notes and newspaper cuttings on the subject.) In his address the Vicar stressed the simplicity of Bob's happy home-life, his love of nature and beauty, his scientific mind ever searching for the truth.

He read from *Corinthians* (2:4:16) which ends, *'For we know that if the earthly frame which houses us today should be demolished, we possess a building which God has provided — a house not made by human hands, eternal and in heaven.'*

Then I felt that Bob was truly alive and with me in the spirit.

I was to learn more of this as the weeks went by . . .

Letters poured in from every quarter. Two remain vividly in my mind, one from a scientist known to Bob for many years: *'Your husband was a great man. In the thirties he was one of the few technocrats looking ahead and he managed to make new apparatus for me that was impossible to make. He led a new way ahead. He has undoubtedly been one of the pioneers of our new scientific knowledge.'*

This thirsting for scientific knowledge was to be shown even more strongly after his death.

The other letter was from a doctor who had worked with Bob on scientific apparatus. He is now a spiritualist.

'. . . Since I have believed, the passing on of friends has taken on an entirely different aspect, and to me all the sting of death has been taken away.'

18

Despite a welter of advice I was determined to stick to the house and garden that Bob and I had so loved, even though much loneliness would lie ahead.

Where can one hide from loneliness, even in a crowded room? Better to be with the things around me that Bob had known and loved, though I had to go through the bitter task of sorting out his clothes. But I did keep his dressing-gown for ever in the bathroom and an old working coat hanging in the kitchen. They were part of his presence about the house. I found them reassuring. It was not a morbid impulse.

I tried to take comfort in the doctor's assurance that had Bob returned home he would have been an invalid for life — that to go the way he did was just what he would have wanted.

The doctor said I was grieving for myself — selfish self-pity, that Bob would have expected me to have the courage to stand on my own two feet.

I tried to steel myself to carry on and take things in my stride. But I simply couldn't. Bob had always been behind me with his practical advice, financial security and sheer warm protective physical presence, shielding me from the world.

Now I was alone.

There were moments when I felt I must end it all. Then in some strange way I would feel his nearness — and his horror at the very idea of my taking a coward's way out.

Slowly the April days gave way to May — our favourite month bright with spring blossoms. The aubretia spread its purple veil round the stone white rabbit and the frog in the rockery. The almond blossom followed the daffodils, then the purple splashes of the honesty and the golden wallflowers. I wandered through the garden, but never seemed to be in it. I managed to struggle through the days, but the evenings were the hardest to bear.

It was then that loneliness stung and I would work and work at papers, solicitors' letters, until I was too tired physically and mentally to do anything more.

And then to bed and the futility of getting up. Time

dragged. The clocks scarcely seemed to move. I tried to dust the house, but still the clocks barely moved. Every second spun out to eternity; every minute, every hour, every day, every week took years to live through.

Time was my enemy, a physical ache that wouldn't go away. All was past, there was no future. Life seemed purposeless. I could not plan. I rose, I crawled through my day. I slept.

I had lost all interest in the world around me. Try as I would to recapture it, I failed. Always the clock. I drifted without aim. There had to be a way back . . .

Like a rock climber pulled back from the brink of disaster by his safety belt, I dangled between hope and despair, filling my diary with appointments for friends to visit me, clinging to them as to a life-line to help me carry through to the next day. I had lost all self-reliance. I felt incomplete, unbalanced, drifting without purpose.

Through the fog I had occasional glimpses of daylight and sanity. Like the day my brother came, bringing a breath of fresh air. We looked at the blue tits' nesting-boxes. I actually laughed for the first time at the antics of his grandchildren.

These were the highlights of my life when I had a shoulder to lean on.

Just as one takes stepping stones across a stream, so I existed on the helping hands of friends and relations — until that weekend . . . when Bob came back to me.

2   Past communications

What I am about to relate now has so much bearing on later events that I feel it important to set it down here.

As a down-to-earth journalist, in the past I had had no interest whatever in spiritualism. I had never even heard of the Spiritualist Association of Great Britain in Belgrave Square.

But it was in 1960, a few months after the death of my mother, to whom I was devoted, when I was feeling miserable and depressed, that on impulse one day, without saying a word to a soul, I took a train to Victoria.

As soon as I arrived, I went to a telephone kiosk and thumbed through the telephone directory. I found the address and rang to ask for a sitting — or whatever it was one had.

Looking back on it all I'm convinced I was guided there by my mother. Everything fell into place. For instance, I learned later that the regular routine was to make an appointment in advance to avoid disappointment. But I was told a Mr William Redmond would be free in half-an-hour.

I felt rather ridiculous. What did I expect to get out of this? Yet something had seemed to compel me to go.

I was surprised when I first entered the Headquarters of the Spiritualist Association, an elegant building at 33 Belgrave Square, London SW1, to see the number of young people passing through the revolving doors.

First I came into a spacious room in which there was a reception desk giving information about sittings. There are notices of the day's lectures and meetings and copies of

Service, the Association's quarterly Calendar of Events, are obtainable.

Service gives full details of lectures, Members of the Association available for private sittings, the times of Spiritual Healing, Visiting Mediums and dates, times for Demonstrations of Clairvoyance, and religious services on Sundays. It also quotes fees for various courses and sittings, and gives a description of the headquarters, with its chapel, library and restaurant.

On the first floor of the building is a small chapel for private meditation, and a large lecture hall. Private sittings are held in several small rooms on the second floor.

I went to the reception desk and paid my fee.

As I waited on a bench at the top of the stairs, Mr Redmond came and asked my name and took me to a small room in which were a table and two chairs.

As I sat down he turned to get a glass of water and then, seating himself opposite me, said:

'Oh dear! I feel you are in such trouble. I do hope we can help you.'

He took a long look at me and asked for something to hold. I gave him my mother's wedding ring which I just happened to be wearing instead of my own.

Mr Redmond said I was in great mental distress. (This was true — I was practically on the verge of a nervous breakdown.) He gave a minute and accurate description of my mother — of my father as well — and said:

'You're full of remorse because she died in a nursing home. You blame yourself, but your mother says it was the only thing possible.'

He spoke of my sister but said *I* was the worrier. (This my mother had often said herself.)

Rather surprisingly he identified the ring as my mother's though, he said, I was married, and she had a special message for my husband.

'Your mother wishes me to say how grateful she is for the care he took of her after your father's death. That he was more than a son-in-law and that she knew he would turn up trumps!'

It might indeed have been my mother speaking for this was precisely the thing she said many a time when she was alive.

Mr Redmond then tossed off various names which I recognised as childhood friends of my mother's. He mentioned all her sisters' names, and said my mother was holding a pug dog called Tony (which we had had as children). Finally he said how happy Mother was to be in touch with me.

I suddenly felt carefree. I walked on air as I went back to Victoria station. This elation enveloped me like a soft cloud all the way home and into the house, where I set about getting our evening meal ready.

Bob came straight into the kitchen as usual, flung his despatch-case on the dresser and looked hard at me.

'My dear, you're looking a different woman! Have you been up to the Press Club?' He'd been urging me to go to London for weeks.

I gave a guarded, 'No'. I felt I couldn't bear any criticism or derision from him.

'Then where *have* you been?' he persisted.

Reluctantly I said: 'I couldn't bear it if you laugh.'

'But why should I?'

He became serious then and listened intently to my story, I ended by saying:

'It was like having a long-distance talk with her.'

Bob said, thoughtfully: 'I just don't understand. But it must have been a wonderful experience.'

I had an appointment with my doctor the next day. When I walked in he looked up and stared at me.

'*What* have you been doing with yourself? You're a different woman — your walk — your face — your bearing —'

Although I still wanted to hug my secret to myself I said at last:

'I've — I've had a long-distance communication — with my mother! I know now she's alive and with me.'

His eyes never left my face as I told him of my sitting with Redmond.

'You don't need *me* any more,' he said when I came to the end. 'I only wish I had more time to go into all this in depth.'

There were several occasions in her lifetime when my mother had shown her acute sixth sense. Once when away from home I couldn't sleep until four in the morning. I just knew I had to go to her. When I arrived unexpectedly at noon she opened the door, showing no surprise, and said: 'I'm not surprised to see you. I was awake until 4 a.m. worrying about you!'

On another occasion, when on holiday in Cornwall, I had left my mother and father to return to our lodgings while I climbed a steep hill to look for a beauty spot. I found it quicker than I had expected and, returning to the top of the hill, saw my parents as two tiny figures, far below me, plodding their way home.

'Oh! Do wait for me!' I called in my mind and, to my surprise, saw them turn and retrace their steps. To my delight, I rejoined them at the foot of the hill.

'Whatever made you return?' I asked.

'I heard you calling me,' said my mother, 'and felt you were in trouble.'

From now on I no longer felt separated from my mother. Whenever I wanted to chat I went to the Spiritualist Association and sat with a medium. I knew none of them but simply chose a name at random.

Every sitting except one was satisfactory, but that one was on a damp thundery afternoon and I felt restless. Simply nothing came through — and my fee was returned. However, the following week I had a splendid session with the same medium.

Every time I went to the Spiritualist Association some little detail of my daily life — which couldn't be coincidence — would come out in the sittings. The time, for instance, when the medium, Mrs St George, spoke of my sitting in a room, with papers and books strewn all over the table, near my mother's portrait. In fact I had done just that the day before, in my study.

Then the time when she said my mother spoke of my

being a good cook — making a beef stew the previous night and naming all the ingredients.

'You couldn't taste it, but it was all right!'

Since I had at the time lost my sense of taste and smell, this was perfectly true.

Bob had gradually become keenly interested in my sittings and sometimes even came with me.

Once, at a sitting with Mrs Ray Welch (formerly Miss Ray Tasker) he was impressed when she told him he had a gold hunter watch belonging to his grandfather which he never used.

My mother had been a talented needlewoman, making all her own children's clothes. When her home broke up she wanted me to keep her old treadle sewing-machine. This she often mentioned at the sittings.

As for me I'd never made a garment in my life, but after she died, to my own surprise and Bob's, I started making my own clothes.

On one occasion the medium told me, 'Your mother says you are having difficulty with a green linen skirt. Try it again and she'll help you with the placket.'

True enough, I'd had trouble with the zip, but that day I went home to tackle it and it went in perfectly!

And so it went on with other dressmaking problems.

By now, if I lost anything Bob would say partly in jest, but also partly in earnest, 'Ask Mother,' and I realised he was beginning really to take an interest in spiritualism.

Because of this I deliberately brought up the subject one evening at dinner when we were entertaining two scientists. They were polite but incredulous.

'What do *you* think?' they asked Bob.

I knew he was in a cleft stick. If he sided with them he knew I'd be hurt and feel 'betrayed', but he would be brave indeed if he differed from their scepticism.

He thought for a long time. Then he said:

'I only know my wife's not a liar — and she's not the most unmechanically-minded woman in the world!'

Then he brought up the incident of the belt on the

sewing-machine. My mother at one sitting had warned that it was frayed.

'I didn't say anything to my wife,' Bob went on, 'but before going to bed I went in her sewing-room to investigate. It *was* frayed, and I repaired it.'

Then I knew Bob *was* really interested in spiritualism in a scientific way.

I still have the first letter Bob wrote to me, just after we had met. I must have written to him, teasingly, saying that he had quite a different type of mind from my own. He replied in a joking way — with rather heavy humour: 'I indignantly refute the suggestion that I have a "destroying, unbelieving type of mind"! I have NOT. Of all men I am the most credulous — when there is adequate foundation to my belief. I have a mechanistic, departmentalised type of mind, a mind in which there has been but little place, so far, for the warmer, cultural things, but definitely not a mind consciously set against belief. I will concede the one but not the other!'

Bob was a man of great strength of character and will-power. What he intended to do he would do, no matter what the obstacles. This he proved right up to the end. For example, the day he was told by his doctor that he had suffered a coronary and must go to hospital, he insisted on driving the car home from the surgery himself — then climbing three flights of stairs to fetch his case, determined to pack it himself ready to be taken to the hospital.

Then when he was due to come home — the day before Christmas Eve — the solid fuel central heating packed up. The water was cold, the fire practically out! I had climbed to the top of the house to inspect the ball-cock, which seemed all right. But what was I to do? This was no time to expect the engineers to come — although I pleaded over the telephone. I told them it was a matter of life and death.

Even as I spoke I felt I was being watched, and looked up. Bob was there — the ambulance had brought him and I hadn't heard him come in. And I had wanted so much to be there to welcome him back!

He took charge at once — he was already half-way up

the stairs — and after a coronary! Then he was down again to inspect the boiler and clear out the fire-box. In vain I pleaded with him, but that will of his was not to be thwarted.

'You've had more than enough to cope with on your own,' he said. 'Now I'll take over.'

Because he was a scientist he was strictly practical and would not accept anything until it was proved. Yet he had a questing and open mind, though he was tolerant of other people's views even when he did not agree with them.

3 First whispers

I had always known my cousin to be psychic and interested in spiritualism although, in those far off days, I had never taken her very seriously. She was strong-minded, placid and comforting and I looked forward to her company.

It was one of those enchanting May week-ends when the garden was full of beauty. Daffodils and early spring flowers had vanished but the purple and white lilacs were flaunting their glory and the air was flooded with birdsong.

It was just a few short weeks after Bob's funeral and though I walked in the garden, its loveliness evaded me.

We sat around the fire that evening, for the nights were still chilly, and the curtains were drawn. I sat listlessly half-reading a book in my favourite chair when my cousin suddenly confided:

'You know, I was dreading coming to this house — because of the loneliness. But it's *not* lonely. Bob's presence floods every part of it. He is here. All over the house. In this very room. I could almost talk to him, if I had something of his to hold.'

Incredulous, I put down my book.

'Can you see him?' I asked.

'I think I could if I held something.'

I almost fell up the stairs in my haste, wondering what I could give her. I found his hair brushes.

She sat there quietly holding them.

'He is standing here, by the settee,' she said. 'He's smiling.' And she started to talk to him.

I felt tremors of excitement passing through me.

At first the sceptical journalist in me dismissed the whole thing as pure imagination. She was trying to humour me. Make me feel better. But the messages she gave me were so real, so like Bob, that I went weak at the knees and started to tremble.

'You must feel him,' she said, and laughed at one of his remarks. 'His personality is so strong. He's coming towards you and now he's stroking your hair.'

Whether it was excitement or imagination I don't know, but I felt a strange electric exhilaration, a current flowing through me. My heart pounded against my ribs, my mouth went dry. Yet at the same time I was filled with a strange and wonderful peace.

'He has been with you since the time he passed, but he couldn't make any impression on you because of your thick veil of grief,' she said. 'Your grief hurts him, my dear. But do try to realise he is with you wherever you go.'

After that, on every evening of her short stay, we 'talked' with Bob by the hearth. I was still a long way from beginning to understand the implications, but a weight seemed to have been lifted from my heart.

For the first time since he had left me I felt comforted — yet doubly unhappy. For I knew it could be only a passing relief from my weight of misery, that when my cousin went from the house Bob would go too. Despite the long communication with my mother, I was still too bereaved and shocked to believe that it might be possible for me to communicate with Bob.

I said to my cousin on the day she left:

'Now I shall be alone for you are taking Bob with you.'

'Nonsense!' she protested. 'His personality is so strong I feel you could talk to him yourself. Just take a paper and pencil and sit quite still and I am sure he will communicate.'

I thought she was just trying to comfort me on her departure, and tried to dismiss the idea from my mind.

Bob and I had led fairly ordinary — some would say humdrum — lives. Our interests away from our respective careers revolved around our friends and our home.

It was, and still is, a beautiful house, planned with love. It was filled with plants and light, and the lovely old period pieces we searched for together over the years, delighting in our bargains.

I had my sewing-room where I would treadle away on my mother's old sewing-machine — now eighty years old!

Bob was always active. I well remember before his coronary begging him to sit down with me in the afternoons. But he was always busy, either with his scientific work as a consultant — making long telephone calls from his groundfloor study — or busying himself with five or ten-gallon casks in the part of the old stables we called 'the winery', where he brewed home-made wine on a vast scientific scale, just for the fun of it. My dear Bob — so wonderfully energetic in spite of an artificial right leg. His car was his one means of locomotion, and he fussed over it as though it were a child!

A perfectionist in all things, he once said to me, 'I don't want you to be just a driver — but a *good* driver.'

He was a good driver himself — an Advanced Motorist — a fact of which he was extremely proud although, typically, he never displayed the badge.

When the weather was good we'd both be in the garden — we were proud of our achievements and loved walking around it, sharing in this or that horticultural triumph.

I did the usual chores and shopping, and in the ordered pattern our lives had assumed, often on winter days we would sit in the firelight in the late afternoon, happy in each other's company.

I was sitting quietly alone before the fire the following Sunday on my return from church, trying to read, my mind as always filled with Bob.

Suddenly the desire to communicate overwhelmed me. The idea was absurd, yet the urge so strong. I picked up a pencil and grabbed the back of an old magazine.

For a few minutes nothing happened. Then I felt the pencil moving, slowly, very slowly, as though making circles. In some strange way I felt comforted and less lonely.

I cannot say the pencil was writing automatically — and yet *I* was not guiding it in any way, as with an effort it moved jerkily across the page. I sat still with my eyes closed. I felt letters were being traced, but they did not make sense . . .

'Is that you, Bob?' I asked in my mind.

I felt the answering scrawl was a big 'Y' followed by 'es'. I sat motionless and the word 'yes' repeated itself several times.

'But this is wonderful!' I thought, as the previous squiggles formed themselves into words all joined together and I sensed, with my eyes shut, the words 'I love you' scrawled across the page.

I opened my eyes and could just read the faint almost illegible outline. I felt a great surge of joy. I raced to the telephone trembling with excitement, and rang my sister.

'Bob has spoken to me!' I cried. 'I don't know how or why, but he's writing on the back of a magazine. He is so close I feel as though I have been talking to him.'

She could be forgiven for thinking me out of my mind, for my sister is a very practical person.

'That's very nice for you, dear,' she said soothingly — as if to a child awakened from a dream — and changed the subject.

After that I 'wrote' every evening using old scraps of paper. I would ask questions mentally, later writing them down to keep a record. Then I would wait for the answers to come tumbling out through the moving pen.

How did I know it was not just my own thought patterns or subconscious answering?

For many months I was plagued with self-doubt, torturing myself. Perhaps I really *was* going mad.

But, for a start, there was a tremendous difference between my own, neat, precise handwriting and the large erratic scrawls on the paper — the messages I was convinced came from Bob.

From that time on I gave up writing in pencil on odd

scraps of paper. I wanted to have a true record of our conversations, and I began to use a pen and notebooks.

As our talks became more fluent I learned that he would be taking 'courses' to enable him to communicate more easily by using other methods. The courses always seemed to take place between sundown and sunrise.

On one occasion, while visiting my sister, just as the sun was going down I felt this strong urge to 'talk' to Bob and snatched up pen and paper — in spite of her saying, 'Let's have supper first — you can do it later.

Sometimes so strong was the compulsion — it always happened at sundown — that once when out driving I had to stop the car by the wayside to write down the message.

In times of stress I could not get through to him, yet *he* knew I was unhappy; for when one evening I did 'reach' him he wrote, 'I was so distressed to see you like that. You should now be cured knowing we can communicate. I am not dead. I am looking forward to seeing you again.'

When I complained of being unable to touch him, to hear his voice, he said he understood my feelings . . . 'It is as though you were trying to imagine I'm still alive. I am not, my dear. I've passed on ahead and we are blessed in having this amazing communication . . . I am very satisfied and so should you be.'

I told him again and again of my loneliness, but Bob said to stop deluding myself that had he recovered all would have been as before. 'I should have been a cripple with a groggy heart. It would have been untold misery for me,' he wrote.

He pointed out that not only I but also he had had to make changes. 'We cannot go on for ever without changes — but they are all for our good. Hard for you. Easier for me.'

We always ended our sessions with prayers of thanksgiving and pleas for care and guidance.

These talks became part of my life.

Our Vicar, so sympathetic and broad-minded, came one evening and sat with me when I was 'communicating', bringing a list of questions. Bob's replies came so fast I hadn't time to write them down, but the gist was that he had now progressed so far that he could communicate in future without the help of the 'Master'. Bob had died so suddenly that he hadn't realised he was dead until he saw his parents and mine. Seeing my sorrow and loneliness he had wanted to re-enter his body, but — always practical — knew he *must* get in touch with me. My grief at first blocked this, but with his Master's help and close study of communications and collaboration ('with brains far superior to mine,' he said) he was now able to get through.

Later the whole process was to develop much more dramatically, but for the present I was more content than I had been for a long time.

My joy knew no bounds when on 24th May in that sad spring he wrote: 'Please don't worry any more, now you know that I am with you. Nothing can stop our relationship. My plans are well-made and now you have nothing to worry about.' As always he signed himself off, 'Love, Bob.'

Even in the most practical ways I was having proof of Bob's guidance and thought for me. Business problems, questions about investments and selling shares, and tax-questions to which I could not possibly have found the answers alone, and he would advise me.

For instance, I was asked to hand in his motor insurance certificate and could not find it. I did not even know what it looked like. In despair I rang the insurance company who told me it was a small piece of paper printed in black, usually carried in the driver's wallet. I searched his wallet. It was not there. In panic I thought I must have left it in his car which I had sold.

'Look in a pigeon hole in my desk,' came into my head as clear as a bell. Call it coincidence — there is no scientific proof — but afterwards there were too many coincidences for them all to be a trick of my own mind.

I rushed to his study, and in the first pigeon-hole I put my hand in I found the missing document. I would never have thought of looking there myself. It was always in moments of panic and frustration that these strange directives came to me.

On one occasion when I was upset, I switched on the radio to make some sound in the deathly claustrophobic atmosphere of the house. At once a beautiful tenor voice, so like Bob's, shattered the silence. 'Oh, Rest in the Lord, Wait patiently for Him, and He will give thee thy heart's desire,' filled the room.

It was one of Bob's favourite arias from *Elijah* which I had heard him sing so many times in his bath! I felt the panic subside. *Coincidence*? I just happened to turn the radio on at that second. It was very comforting.

Then there was the cheque stub. I had gone to our local electrical shop with some trifling repair and mentioned my husband's death a few months previously. They knew and liked him and after offering condolences mentioned an outstanding bill from the previous winter. 'We didn't like to worry you,' they said, 'knowing of your husband's illness.' By now it was June.

'I have no outstanding bills,' I replied. 'And in any case everything is under Probate. Give me the bill and I will ask my solicitors to pay it,' and this was done.

A few days later, alone in the kitchen at midnight, I was thinking over my financial problems, as Bob had died before reaching pensionable age.

'Look in my cheque book stubs for last November,' came repeatedly and insistently into my mind.

I had a good idea of where to find them but felt too tired to make the effort. Anyhow, what was the point?

The message was repeated again and again. Like a sleep-walker I crossed to Bob's desk. I turned the entries until I reached November. I couldn't believe my eyes. There was the stub entry on 13th November. I found the cheque had been cleared in December. The electrical shop refunded the money.

In those dark days of despair these little reminders of Bob's presence brought warmth and comfort.

As the rose-scented June days passed and the peonies and poppies flaunted their brave colours, so every evening I now wrote to Bob. 'Go on writing to me and I will always reply,' he told me. 'I will help you and it gives me great pleasure, for I want you to be happy. I was so sorry for you to have to carry on alone and I will make myself go with you wherever you go until we meet again.'

Yet in spite of the comfort these daily sessions brought me, at this stage I was in an agony of doubt. At a point when I began to question my own sanity I asked Peter, a young scientist friend of Bob's who had worked with him on several projects, if he would come and give me his opinion. This he did on 27th June 1971. We started our session.

At once Bob expressed delight at 'seeing' his old friend. 'Peter is a very strong force. You and I and he are on the same wavelength. He is interested in the same means of communication, which I'd like to explain to him. I can pass my thoughts through your pen and you can pick them up. You're much in my mind as I am in yours — that's why I can come to you any time and anywhere.'

His Master had praised him as a good pupil who had made great strides in communication owing to his scientific and spiritual nature, and to the great love we have for each other. Though he could guide my thoughts, he could not foresee the future.

'My job is to look after you, and follow those things that interest me.'

When Peter asked him his future intentions, Bob replied that it could be chemistry or bio-chemistry or possibly electronics. His Master said he could go far. 'At the moment I am at your side. I see Peter lounging in his chair. Only a hair's-breadth separates us. I can touch you but you're not aware of it.'

Answering Peter's questions he assured him of his happiness — with just one regret: the absence of his wife. Those on the other side who were less happy and restless had not yet come to terms with their new state, for instance those who had died suddenly from an accident.

From the personal, Bob passed to world affairs. 'I do not like the way things are shaping up — the massing together of Great Powers. Unless there is a spiritual awakening there will be ruin.'

He could be in two places at the same time, he said.

'Can you recognise the places?'

'What a silly question. Of course I do!'

I could almost hear his chuckle.

And what would happen to me when I died, I asked him. Again he said, 'Don't be silly. We'd be together as on earth.'

He knew the sun was shining where we were and said what a pity it was we were both indoors. Where he was, there was no day or night — just, 'a diffused light'.

Peter asked him whether various religions mattered, for instance, Buddhist and Christian, to which Bob replied, 'Not at all. If one is true to the precepts of one's religion one is growing upwards. It is the pattern of life that good must overcome evil and to that end all religions turn. It is so difficult to try and make people on earth realise this and it is no good trying to explain.'

Asked if there was evil on his plane and, if so, how he fought it, Bob replied, 'Yes. It is very strong and is overcome by prayer and thought.'

'How do you recognise it?' asked Peter.

'By its very nature. Man is still evil, even when he dies, and the evil still clings to him until he can advance upwards.'

Peter asked whether help could be given and Bob replied that help was given by means of teachers.

'Do you mean like Christ?' Peter persisted.

'Yes, I do,' replied Bob. 'Only Christ was above this level and tried to help the whole of mankind.'

Bob also said they had visitors from higher planes whose work was to try and raise up those who needed help, bringing the message of goodwill towards all men. Peter asked Bob whether he was protected from evil.

'Of course,' Bob replied. 'You know that I believe in God and He can afford protection to all. It was not necessary for me to go through all the lower stages of training. So much depends on your own state of mind when you pass over. The man who has the good of his neighbour at heart is much more fitted for advancement than the selfish type'.

To close the talk Peter then put some scientific questions which I could not follow, but he thought the replies were very significant.

As I laid my pen down on the table I asked Peter what he thought of the interview and he said he was convinced that it was Bob 'talking' through me, as he had been watching me closely all the time and that *I* could not have thought out the replies so quickly.

4 Practical help

In all sorts of every-day, practical ways Bob made me feel I was not alone, that he was with me always to help and guide me.

He was the one who had always managed our financial and other affairs, bringing his precise mind to bear on all the details.

Now I had to make my own decisions, often about matters I'd never handled in my life before. Yet it was astonishing that in moments of perplexity I always seemed to find the right answer, as if inspired.

Friends were amazed at my ability to handle the estate, knowing how unpractical I was.

I refused to leave the house — the home we had made so lovingly together — although in our 'talks' Bob had assured me again and again that if I wanted to move he would be with me to life's end. But for me it was always my home — our home — and it seemed to welcome me back whenever I'd been away.

Some of his advice concerned trivial things — some, of course, important. But now I'd grown quite used to calling on him for help.

There were still moments of anguish, though, of such deep depression that I longed for his physical presence, to be able to see him, touch him. Yet at such times I was buoyed up by the evidence of his guidance, even in the smallest problems that he would easily have settled himself.

One such concerned the payment of £5 from a woman who had bumped into my car when it was stationary, damaging the bumper. She had admitted the fault was hers and promised to pay up for the repair — but her husband kept making excuses for not doing so. What was I to do? It would be absurd to take the matter to court.

Suddenly the thought came into my mind:

'Get Harry to go along and collect it.'

At that same moment Harry — a helper of Bob's and mine and a good and trusted friend — turned up and I told him my problem.

'Give me their name and address,' he said, grinning, 'I'll be back in ten minutes.'

And he was — with the cheque!

Then there was the incident of the Grandfather clock. Our house is full of antique clocks — they were one of Bob's hobbies and he had a special set of watchmaker's tools to keep them in order. Every Saturday morning there was the ceremony of winding the clocks! *I'd* never been allowed to touch them when he was alive. Now all I could do was wind them up and hope for the best.

Grandfather had stopped, the exquisitely wrought-iron hour-hand blocking the keyhole and pointing at 8, the minute-hand at 12. I was afraid if I moved the hour-hand I might upset the striking mechanism. What could I do?

'Set the pendulum in motion,' came into my mind repeatedly.

How could I when the clock had stopped?

I turned my back on it, but the words persisted. So I opened the clock door and swung the pendulum. At once the clock struck eight, so now I was able to move the hand without upsetting the chimes and get at the keyhole!

Then there was the incident of the kitchen clock and the decorators. This is a tall American (first mass-produced) clock which lives on the high mantelpiece in the kitchen. To reach it I have to climb the kitchen steps. It has a right-angled key about 1½ inches long.

In readiness for the decorators I climbed up and lifted the clock down on to the table, laying the key by its side.

When they were leaving that afternoon I saw they had replaced the clock on the mantelpiece so I climbed the steps to find the key to wind it. It wasn't there.

I asked the painters where they had put it. They looked surprised.

'Never seen it.' And they made for the back door.

'But I must have it to start the clock up. I left it on the table,' I insisted.

In a hurry to be off they searched the kitchen, still declaring they'd never seen it, but to no purpose.

'You *must* have moved it,' I cried, glancing at the top of the clock which nearly reached the ceiling, impossible for me to get at.

All at once I shouted: 'Look on *top* of the clock!' The thought had suddenly come to me. I hardly recognised my voice.

They looked at each other as though I were crazy.

'On the *top*?' They both looked incredulous and moved again to the door.

'Look on the top!' I repeated twice over.

As though humouring a spoilt child, the taller of the two, still grinning at his mate, climbed the steps and fumbled along the top of the clock. His expression changed as he held out the key to me. 'Whatever made you say that?' he asked in a subdued voice. 'I certainly don't remember putting it there.'

I smiled. 'I think it was my husband who told me.'

They probably thought me mad!

I seemed to be having trouble with all the clocks. All at the same time, something went wrong with the French clock, the Westminster chimes and Grandfather. I sent for a clock-smith — who had never met my husband.

When he had put everything right he came into the kitchen for payment.

He smiled at me. Then he said an astonishing thing:

'I've a feeling your husband's been standing over me all the time I've been touching his clocks. Particularly with Grandfather. I found a note pasted on the inside, 'Oiled Nov. 1967'. I felt he was telling me that was all the old boy needed — just a drop of oil.'

I told him that I, too, was often aware of my husband's presence.

Then came a further surprise. He said he was psychic, too!

No one had ever been allowed to touch Bob's filing cabinet. Even when he was in hospital and I'd offered to file the huge pile of letters that had collected for him, he said:

'Please don't. I'll deal with them myself when I get home.'

So when one June day I had to find some essential Income Tax papers, I looked where I'd have expected them to be — filed under 'Income Tax'. But they were not there.

Short of going through the whole cabinet I'd no idea where to look. It was an urgent matter and I was completely frustrated. I wracked my brain to imagine where the papers could be.

Then, I don't know why, I reached for a file labelled 'Building Societies' — and there were the documents I was looking for.

Coincidence?

The following September another strange thing happened. This time my accountants had asked for papers recording what Bob had spent on restoring the house — over fifteen years ago. They needed them to make a tax claim.

It was a challenge. Bob would have known at once where they were. But where could *I* look?

I spent a whole morning going through all the possible folders: repairs, house . . . Defeated — I really couldn't go through *all* the files individually — I was just about to close the study door on my frustration when the message leaped into my mind:

'Look into my 'Dead Income Tax' file.'

It sounded absurd. I'd been meaning to throw out that file for months, feeling it must now be obsolete. Yet something always held me back.

Saying to myself how ridiculous and hopeless it was to expect to find papers dealing with Bob's affairs of 15 years ago (and why in an Income Tax file?), nevertheless I found the file and opened it.

And there, among copies of Income Tax returns for 1956, was the carbon copy of a 3-page letter Bob had written to the accountants giving details of all the expenses incurred during the house restoration, and enclosing receipted bills.

I could never have come across those papers by chance.

So many other apparently silly little incidents occurred: The time I mislaid some flower photos and a 'voice' said, 'Look under your handbag on the kitchen dresser,' where indeed I looked — and found them tucked out of sight.

Then the day in my cottage in Deal when I was looking for a tin of zinc ointment in the medicine cupboard. There was no sign of it.

'Look in the broom cupboard,' came clearly to my mind.

So under the stairs I looked, fumbling in the dark, and there it was, though when and why I put it there I've no idea!

And now, all these years after Bob's death, putting these pages together I wished I had a stapler. I didn't know that Bob had ever had one. Yet on impulse I went into his study, walked over to his desk, put out my hand — and found one!

5   The search for proof

In spite of all the 'evidence', doubts still persisted in my mind. One moment I'd be up in the air, the next plunged in depths of depression. Wondering . . . Wondering if it was all in my mind, my imagination.

It was clear the time had come to seek scientific and professional advice and guidance about my 'conversations' with Bob.

It was on a day of despondency that I sat by the telephone feeling I must get in touch with someone interested in the occult, who would perhaps be sympathetic.

I first rang the College of Psychic Studies, and got on to someone who was kind and helpful, as briefly I outlined my story, explaining that I thought I was in communication with my husband, but that it was by thought, and certainly not 'automatic writing'.

To my relief she showed no surprise. She pointed out that it must be 'inspirational writing' — obviously not unheard of.

Thus encouraged I rang the Society for Psychical Research and the Churches Fellowship for Psychical and Spiritual Studies. I made all these calls on impulse on the same morning, and all gave the same rather vague reply.

I then bought a booklet by that excellent medium, Ursula Roberts, *Hints on Mediumistic Development*. Thumbing through it, I came upon a chapter where Mrs Roberts emphasises the difference between automatic writing and inspirational writing. It was the first time I had seen any mention in print of inspirational writing, which she said was the centre of activity in the medium's mind.

'. . . each word or sentence is known in the mind before it is transmitted through the hand,' she wrote. 'The link between hand, brain and spirit operator often becomes so perfect that the medium finds it difficult to describe whence the communication originated.'

The strange events that had been happening since Bob's death now seemed to be forming themselves into a pattern and I desperately wanted proof from a third party, if possible a medium.

Bob was lying very ill in St Olave's Hospital the last time I'd sat with a medium before his death. It had been my mother's anniversary, the 22nd February 1971.

I had booked the appointment two months before with (the late) Nora Blackwood, at a time when Bob seemed to be recovering.

Her first words startled me.

'A man has come to you in spirit. It is your husband.'

'No! Not my husband!' I said, shaken, knowing too well how desperately ill he was.

'Then it is your father who is so close to you at this time,' she continued, 'for your husband is seriously ill.'

Then to my intense amazement she gave an accurate description of his medical condition.

'He has a damaged heart. Circulation is slow. He has no energy and he is *not* co-operating. Clots. There are clots in the aorta. His loving spirits could help him when asleep — but he is so self-determined he is difficult to help. The blood is flowing now but the arteries are thickening.' Then: 'He must put the brake on, and adopt wise living.'

She told me my mother was there and was saying Bob was too impatient to rest.

'Your husband is a scientist,' the medium said, 'always working under great pressure. He's a good man — but not every one can get on with him, or understand him.'

This was true.

She then said he was about 60 and would have to take tablets for the rest of his life.

'You're talking about a bungalow,' she said, (this also was true) 'but he *must be careful*.' She stressed this again and again.

'His spirit is willing but the flesh is weak. It is such foolish behaviour on his part — in future there must be no lifting, and no stairs.'

I asked if he would come home again.

'*If he is careful* — but it will be all of a month. It's like asking too much of an old car. Your husband should recognise this and go slow.'

Actually it *was* just a month when, so much better, he was due to come home. But he overdid things and died in his sleep.

I went straight to the hospital after the sitting and found Bob anxious to know if it had been a good one. Keeping it on as light a plane as I could, I said:

'It was quite extraordinary — she might have been a doctor! She gave a perfect diagnosis of your condition.'

I then told him how she had insisted he must go slow and be more co-operative.

Later, in his diary I found an entry for that day recording that I'd come in, 'after first-class session with spiritualist about me.'

He was obviously very impressed and interested.

It was on 14th May that same year, about six weeks after Bob's death that I had my next sitting with a medium.

During those early days of our inspirational talks I'd asked Bob whether he would be there if I went to a medium.

He replied: 'Yes. I will come along with my Master.'

(This was before he had managed his 'talks' on his own.)

After failing to make an appointment with three of the mediums I'd sat with previously, I was able finally to arrange a sitting with Mrs Ray Welch.

I felt utterly worn and broken as I entered the Spiritualist Association.

Mrs Welch came towards me as I entered the room, saying I had brought a man with me.

'Such power! Such love! Such a strong personality — like a bear hugging you. Your husband has only recently passed over. He was sad at leaving you so suddenly but delighted at the way you are coping.'

Then she said: 'He doesn't want to be just a communicator — but a *good* communicator. He is studying at the Halls of Learning.'

The expression was so typical of Bob. I remembered his comment about my learning not just to be a driver but a *good* driver.

At one point Mrs Welch seemed puzzled. 'I see a bridge,' she said, 'between two lakes. A bridge! A link! There is communication between you.'

She still seemed bewildered but I understood at once for she couldn't know that, before the sitting, I had asked Bob to tell me, through a third person, that we *were* communicating in some way.

Mrs Welch continued: 'You have a beautiful garden and home. He is interested in the garden.' Many mediums have told me this. 'And often walks there,' she continued. 'There was no great passion between you, just good companionship with mutual respect. You were partners. He had been working in London, and then partly retired.'

She even mentioned he had been a Director of a Board but a pension agreement had not been settled at the time of his death. (This was all so completely accurate.)

'He passed with heart trouble,' she went on. 'It was as well, otherwise he would have been a cripple for life and could not have borne it. You would have been an old woman before your time. You have got rid of all his clothes except a dressing-gown that hangs on his bathroom door. You have only one decent photograph of him but many snaps.' She was uncannily accurate.

Laughing, Mrs Welch said he was holding out, of all things, a cane carpet beater of the old-fashioned type, and joking about it. I recognised this at once as one he had bought not long before at a junk shop — which had annoyed me at the time!

She mentioned Bob's right leg and said she felt great pain

there. I told her it had been amputated above the knee.

She then said an extraordinary thing.

'I see your husband very clearly, a jovial sort of man, and my guide tells me that I have met him in the flesh — but I don't recognise him.'

(In fact Bob and I had indeed sat together with Mrs Welch when she was Miss Tasker. When I told her, she laughed and said: 'That was over ten years ago, yet my guide insisted I had met him before.'

It was an unforgettable experience. Every incident Mrs Welch had described was true. I felt Bob's presence just as though I was lifted up out of my body, of having really communicated with the old, cheerful Bob, whom I loved so much.

'Your husband's power is so strong,' she said as we finally shook hands. 'If only I had the time I could go on talking for hours.'

Some time previously before my 'writing' started, I had been feeling so wretchedly ill and miserable that I'd arranged a Healing Session on the third floor of the Spiritualist Association building.

But this sitting had been so amazing, so comforting, that I cancelled the Healing Session and left the building feeling light-hearted and filled with renewed belief that Bob really was with me.

On 1st December 1971, 8 months after Bob's death, I sat with Kathleen St George. This time my mother and father came through first and spoke of the happy Christmasses we'd had together. Then Bob joined them. The medium said:

'He passed over only a few months ago. He has such a strong personality . . . He always had a neatly-folded handkerchief in his top pocket.' It had to be changed every day!

As other mediums had emphasised, she said how he was shaken at his sudden passing. Then she mentioned my father's Sussex ancestry, how charming my mother was, yet with a strong sensible personality, that I had only one

47

photo of my husband, small things in themselves. Then:

'Such a strong bond of affection and understanding binds you together!'

It was quite fantastic to hear from her details of our home which she said Bob was telling her — details personal and intimate. She described the garden, the greenhouse, trees, birds, Bob's bird-table. But the most remarkable was her reference to the oleander plant — quite unusual — which Bob had bought at a sale the previous year.

Then the medium spoke of the peaceful setting of the house: 'There is an antique table in the hall, that belonged to your mother. There are two lights burning in the sitting-room. And you have a live coal-fire.' Of all things, she even mentioned planks that could be lifted into place in the coal-shed to keep the coal in, and cupboards in the sitting-room at eye level.

So, call it coincidence, telepathy, anything you like, but what all the mediums spoke about only confirmed what Bob was constantly telling me in his 'talks' — that he was able to describe through third parties, who'd never even known him, all the details of our home, our life together and his personality.

Yet I still was not satisfied. From notes I took at the time, in moods of abject depression, I can see I was still seeking *proof*.

As the Old Year gave place to the New and I fell into another 'slough of despond', Bob suddenly suggested I should seek another sitting with a medium.

Two months previously when I was at the Spiritualist Association, a striking-looking young man had passed me in the hall. I noted his startlingly blue eyes. So struck was I that I asked if he was a medium. He said he was and gave his name as David Young.

I called after him: 'One day I would like to sit with you!'

It was on 12th January 1972, that I rang the Association and asked for a sitting with David Young. I expected to get an appointment right away, but the earliest he could see me was a week later, on the 19th January.

In view of the extraordinary happenings that followed

this sitting, I must record here the 'conversation' I had with Bob that afternoon.

I told him how I had hoped to see David Young the next day, but the following Tuesday was the best he could do.

'Yes. I would rather you sat with someone of our choosing,' Bob replied. 'I can concentrate on coming through him — a very good idea of yours and mine. It suddenly came to me that you needed proof again after being so much on your own. You need reassurance and he can give it to you.'

Then for the first time I put into words the thought that for so long had been running through my head.

'Will you try to get him to say we communicate? Let a third person, unknown to us, say that we are communicating and I will take it as a proof, and really believe!'

In my hastily scrawled notes made at the time, and not even relying on my memory, I have the words: 'Yes. I will do my best to get across. Sorry it's not tomorrow but on second thoughts it's too much for you — you'd be exhausted. Far better go up quietly on Tuesday — and I will demonstrate.'

And what an amazing sitting it was!

'I speak very quickly if I get through,' David Young explained as we sat down. 'I can promise nothing. If I do not get through it's useless to pursue it — as with my last client at 4 o'clock. I took her down to the Reception Desk to get her money back.'

Even as he had come into the room I knew somehow we were going to be successful. I felt drawn to him, and a great sense of power swept over me.

He began simply: 'I will try. I do not believe in padding messages. If I get through I shall give them just as they come. If I cannot, it is useless to continue.'

He took my hands and then dropped them. I sensed his magnetic power.

'Your husband is here,' he said. 'He passed very quickly. Like a flash. He should have had a degree or award. He is a scientist.'

He spoke so quickly and with such force I could hardly

make notes. I was carried away on an upsurge of Bob's love and nearness.

'He says this is a special effort he has made to prove himself. He had a scientific mind and says you're linked with him in writing. Do you understand?'

I was delighted. I almost shouted for joy. David Young had no idea that this was the very pact Bob and I had made between us before the sitting.

Even as I'd sat in the waiting-room for David's arrival, I kept saying in my mind, 'Please remember our promise, Bob. Tell me through a third person that we are communicating, and I will never doubt again.'

Here, surely, was the proof I had been seeking for a year?

David Young continued: 'Precise detail, great honesty. He went so quickly he never finished his work, which has annoyed him very much. Very keen. Went abroad a lot. Should have been a professor.'

I said, 'Yes. He was devoted to his work and would have continued studying but for our marriage.'

'No children,' he continued, 'but not necessary to you. Says you used to boss him, but that was his heavy joke. Not everyone could live with him. Sympathetic and helpful to everyone. Had an old-fashioned father, and was brought up on old-fashioned principles. Loved you deeply but could never express it, but now wishes he had been able to.'

David then mentioned by name two scientists Bob knew and even the name of the late Chairman of Bob's company.

He went on: 'Laboratories, physicists, together they made a team. No time for red tape. Spoke against injustice. Was liked by many but also made enemies. Was anxious to prove continuity. Was cremated, as he wished. Did not wish for the shedding of crocodile tears at his grave.'

These were the words Bob had actually used to me several years ago when we'd been talking of 'funeral v. cremation'.

Again that great love for me, David emphasised. Bob

was now acting as my guardian and always would. He said we met late in life. That he was simple, sensible, practical and undemonstrative, and wishes I could enjoy myself more.

'How *can* I now that he's gone?' I asked.

Back came the reply, quick as a flash.

'But I haven't gone. I am always with you.'

'But,' I said, 'how can you be with me always when you're so busy and interested in scientific work?'

Bob replied: 'It is so simple but you can't understand. It's a question of fourth dimension.'

I told David that I had put this as a test question because, when I had asked this at home Bob had always given me this same reply.

At this stage David held up a shilling and, laughing, asked:

'Is his name Bob?'

When I nodded he smiled and said, 'That's just what he's saying!' (For those who may have forgotten, or grew up with decimalisation, 'bob' was the slang word for the old shilling.)

All this was a perfect description of Bob's character — a lifelong friend couldn't have described him more accurately. Yet I had never seen David Young before, except for that brief encounter in the hall of the Spiritualist Association, and he had certainly never heard of Bob.

6 Growing closer

By now, a year after Bob's death, I'd become quite used to getting messages from him by our talks and through mediums. I accepted him as a living and vital force, watching over me, guiding my decisions — even driving with me in my little car.

At a difficult junction I'd say, 'Bob, take over. I can't manage this,' and unseen hands seemed to relax the tension in my own while a warning voice usually whispered, 'You're driving much too fast!' I'd slow down at once.

I began to read all the occult-slanted books I could find and learned I wasn't alone in my strange new world. Others — far more gifted than I — had had glimpses of eternal life, had found that where there was love, the 'dead' (I hated the word) really did come back when urgently needed.

I devoured all the books by Geraldine Cummins. I loved her *Swan on a Black Sea*, and that tenderly written *Swan in the Evening*, by Rosamund Lehmann. I was exploring new country, a new dimension.

One night after reading Grace Rosher's *Beyond the Horizon*, just before going to sleep, I asked Bob again whether he would try to get in touch by automatic writing as I'd so dearly love to see his handwriting again.

His reply came back sharply: 'My dear, no! I've told you before I cannot do automatic writing and we already have our excellent method of communication. You're asking too much. Don't you realise that some people have one gift and others another? Remember St Paul to the Corinthians! Some are painters, others enquirers. You are a journalist.

I'm a scientist. You can't excel at half-a-dozen things at once! We've perfected this way of communicating, swift and clear, and we can communicate at any time. Now, dear, for the last time, go to sleep! I shan't answer you again tonight.'

As when he was on earth and I'd ask him something as he turned out his reading light, so now I almost felt him turning his head away and then silence — and only the nearness of his dear presence.

I turned out the light. It was three in the morning and glancing through the window-pane, for the first time in a year, I noticed Orion's glittering belt passing on its way.

Before Christmas Bob had been mentioning that I should get a tape-recorder. This I didn't want to do — I'd have no idea how to work it.

He insisted I should write a book, and a tape-recorder would be so helpful. Then I could talk to him and speak his replies aloud — and this would save the painstaking task of writing down all our conversations.

It was quite true that as Bob's talks grew faster I was so often carried away that I gave up all ideas of keeping written records; I'd just hold the pencil and let it squiggle while we chatted. This method would be far more satisfactory than having to switch off my mind, as it were, while I wrote the message down.

But a tape-recorder? No, said the practical side of me. They're expensive and with my 'unmechanical mind' I was sure I'd never get it to work!

Yet Bob urged me on. So, during Christmas week while I was in Bournemouth I roamed around the large stores and priced them. The exercise daunted me! I was sure I'd never be able to use one, they looked so complicated.

But help was at hand. When I returned home, a young friend who knew all about these machines said he would choose one for me, the simplest and cheapest, and show me how to work it.

So Bob's plan seemed to be working out, as always. Whenever I needed help or encouragement there was always someone at hand to advise me. I was to prove this as Bob's scheme unfolded.

I bought my tape-recorder soon after that first sitting with David Young in January. I found using it so much simpler than trying to write my notes. Bob, too, became more fluent not having to stop every now and then while I caught up on my writing.

My first tape is of great interest because of the questions I asked.

'Talk to *me* now, Bob,' I said. 'Tell me about yourself.'

After a first private chat he said:

'I'm going on a course again but it won't affect you. You'll be asleep. I shall be studying the art of communications again because I think it's so important. I'm also going to do some electronics, and that will interest me very much.'

I asked him if they guided the earth thoughts of other scientists, and he replied:

'Of course we can. That's our job — to help them develop their own faculties. I do wish you were more technically-minded! Then I could explain it to you. But it would be useless — you wouldn't understand a word I was saying.'

I asked him where he was at that moment and he told me he was sitting by my side and was glad that, for once, I was resting quietly.

'There's so much I wanted to ask you,' I said, 'but this is just like seeing you again and I can't even think! What is it like on your plane? Are you above us or around us, or are you with us?'

'We are with you. I'm as close to you as breathing. I'm always close to you, my dear, and you really ought to be able to feel it! You ought to have the moral support of my strength and comfort, for this is what I can give you.'

I asked him to tell me again if his passing was a shock to him.

'Yes. It was a great surprise. I didn't realise at first I'd passed over until I saw your mother and father and my mother and father, and realised that something was peculiar.'

'Did they tell you that you were dead?'

'Yes. They said I'd "joined them".'

I asked what his immediate reaction was.

'To get in touch with you. I felt I *must* get in touch and try to get back into my old body.'

'Could you see your body lying in the hospital bed?'

'Yes! And it looked very strange to me. But I felt, if I could get there I could contact you. But when I found it impossible I enquired how I could communicate with you — it was very difficult, as I've told you before, because of your own grief. It was like a thick veil.'

'Could you see me?'

'Yes. I could see you and what you were doing — and that made me sad because I wanted to tell you I was alive and well and wanted to get in touch. But then it was quite impossible, so I sought the advice of my Master.'

'How did you get in touch with him?'

'He was waiting to receive me and told me he would try to make communication possible. But it would take some time because of your own earth condition. So I had to wait, although I did try and come to you in your sleep.'

I felt this must be true — I'd had such wonderful dreams when I had been in Bob's arms.

I asked him if he had seen my grief all that time.

'Yes. This is one of the most unpleasant things about this so-called death — to see those you love in a terrible state of anxiety and depression. And so I tried all I could to make myself felt and to tell you I wasn't dead but still with you. It seemed impossible — until your cousin, Gwen, came and saw me and spoke to me — and said you would communicate. *She* first put this idea into your head.'

'Could everyone communicate in this way if they wanted to?'

'No. For instance, your own father and mother couldn't — but it was your mother who directed you to the Spiritualist Association as she knew she could communicate in that way.'

'Are they with me as much now as you are?' I asked.

'Not as much. It was rather like our marriage. When you

55

were single you were with them and needed their support. Now we're married you need *my* support and therefore you have it and I'm with you all the time.'

I asked him to tell me more.

'As I've said, you and I are still in our married state. Your father and mother are often with you, but I'm *always* with you — just as we were on earth.'

Would he be with me to the end of my days, I asked him, and he replied that of course he would — it was his duty.

'But yet I'm keeping you back, Bob!'

'You're not. I can carry on with my own work but I can still be with you at the same time. I've told you this before. I can be in two places at once and you're never out of my sight. Whatever you do, wherever you go, I'm with you.'

Then he said: 'You used to say, "I can't go there because it reminds me of Bob". Like your fuss about London Bridge Station. I am not at London Bridge, nor at Nuffield House any more. I'm with *you*. If you go to Deal I am there. Wherever you go, I shall be there too.'

'You mean it's like being possessed by a spirit?'

'If you like. But it's being possessed by a *good* spirit.'

'I feel,' I said, 'as though I'm just talking to you as if you were in the chair beside me. Did you go to church this morning?'

'Yes. I enjoyed the service.'

'And yet you were here at home! This is what I can't understand.'

'No you can't. And I can't explain it. It's the law of nature.'

It was a wonderful and satisfying talk, with me stressing again how he'd still be alive if only he had done what the doctors advised, while Bob pointed out again that he would have been a cripple and confined to the house. God's plan was the right one, he said. He could now carry on his career on *his* plane, and I could get on with my journalism until we met again.

7   Still growing closer

So delighted was I with my new 'toy' that I was immediately anxious to sit with David Young again, taking it with me, to record every word he said. Ten months after Bob's death, on 22nd February 1972, I arranged a second sitting. This date was to be stamped on my memory.

As David Young came into the room he said:

'Your husband is here with tremendous force. Good heavens! The man killed himself by his persistence.'

'That's true,' I replied, 'he was coming home from the hospital, but he overdid things and passed in his sleep. You *are* amazing! Now, let me set up the tape-recorder.'

I sat opposite him with the recorder between us.

He began: 'All I want you to say is "yes" or "no". We're on tape. If I get nothing I shall say so. But as I'm linking here with you very strongly and definitely, I'm seeing and hearing your husband as he comes to you. I feel — a great deal of leg-pulling, a great sense of humour all the time. As he comes to me he gives the name of Robert, but you call him "Bob", and I feel he is linking here. A man of science on earth. A man who did what he wanted to.'

'Very much so!' I answered.

'Nobody would have got a word in edgeways if he didn't want it.'

'Perfectly true.'

'And he's saying to me that he is fulfilling a promise. On earth he was sceptical of spiritualism, but he had an open mind.'

'Exactly!'

'I feel that on earth he did contact spiritualism but

wasn't quite convinced himself. Your mother came back to you at a seance, your husband's telling me. Going back years ago, your mother passed in spirit. You happened to come to London and you happened to come here. Is this correct, please?'

I said it was.

'There was a man here.'

'I sat with a man.'

'And was this Bill Redmond?'

'Yes.'

'Fine!' He chuckled. 'Your husband is saying that it *was* Bill Redmond you sat with. This is well before my time here.' He broke off. 'All right, Bob.'

Then he addressed me again. 'And your mother came and gave you a very evidential message. She had just passed over. You went home and told your husband. I feel he is giving this as conclusive evidence that he's more alive than he has ever been, because — I have to ask you this question, Madam — could I have ever known what your husband has just told me?'

'No!'

David Young then said he wished to 'link' me with cremation and I explained that this concerned my husband.

'Just say "yes" or "no",' the medium said, 'but I feel your husband was cremated. I feel he was quite an engineer in many ways. I don't mean an engineer, literally, but a man who delves into everything. I feel he was very medical.'

'Medically-minded,' I said.

'Yet he dealt with science.'

'Very much so.'

'As though I am in a laboratory. I feel — as though I keep seeing nuclear energy — yet I'm not working on the atom as such, but I was on a chemical link the whole time.'

I confirmed this.

He then spoke of links with Ireland and I told him we'd been to Ireland many times.

'And he's laughing because, though your husband was English, he had a lot of blarney about him!'

'Yes, he liked to pull people's legs!'

'Bob is saying that he now knows without doubt that he's more alive than he's ever been . . . Was never lucky in his communications . . . took very much after his mother . . . He's saying that underneath his hard exterior he was soft . . .'

David Young then started to speak of the country. 'I feel here quite a house, in its own grounds. His favourite room wasn't the lounge but a little room he sat in just off the lounge . . . He's saying to me that it was his "untidy room" and he didn't like you tidying up there. Correct?'

I said it was.

'I'm not seeing any children at all.'

'That's so.'

'No. Yet I'm talking about the boys. Probably his friends. They were like boys to him.'

'Yes.'

'I feel here a great link with the Church of England, but High Church, not Low Church.

Bob had been a chorister for many years.

David Young laughed. He said he had such a sense of joy. Then he mentioned two of Bob's friends, both of whose names began with 'B'. One, a scientist, Dr du Barry Barnett; the other an old-friend and their choir-master, William Ballard. At first the medium was confused over their initials but finally sorted them out.

'I feel a great link with scientific communications here. Your husband is saying that he is still carrying on his scientific research . . . and there is much love for you, I feel. He says you have spoken to friends about all this, but they didn't quite believe you.'

'Some did. Some didn't.'

As other mediums had already noted, he said Bob's death was sudden — quite unexpected. Then he said:

'I keep seeing Surrey — as though I am living in Surrey. There is Richmond, there's Esher. I am going up that way, and don't get it. What I'm seeing here . . . in Surrey, is . . .'

And he mentioned the place where I live. I was amazed.

'I sense a great feeling of laughter from your husband.

He's thinking about Robin Hood. Ah, yes! Your husband would give to people in need. He had — still has — a lot of boyish humour.'

'Yes.'

'My dear, he still has. "You've still got my books and my papers," he says, "but I never completed my papers," and he says he will try in many ways to communicate with you himself.'

'This is what I've asked him to do,' I replied. 'To come through a third person and tell me this is what he is doing. So that I may believe it.'

He asked if I understood this, and I told him I did indeed.

He then said Bob was very much against social injustice; he was a man close to nature, to animals, and that there was a strong feeling that he was trying to communicate with me directly.

'This is what I don't understand. I wish he'd explain!'

David Young then said this is what he felt Bob would try to do, and suggested I should get a sitting with a Mr Leslie Flint, a Direct Voices medium.

'But I do feel from Bob a great deal of love . . . once he got going I felt he could become very excitable — a man who would rather be in his own home but didn't like to be entertained. I feel he had a scar here where my hand is now . . .'

He had put his hand on his right thigh — where Bob had had his right leg amputated.

'I feel as though,' he continued, 'as though I limped a little as well — on my right leg, and I'm getting the feeling of trying to walk, but I'm walking with a little limp. It could be very noticeable at times. Not so much at other times. I feel there is a great love for you, too, and he's saying you have been having impressions — well, that you've been feeling something around you.'

'I feel him,' I said.

'Yes!'

David then gave the names of several relatives of mine who had died. Then he spoke of Poland and a scientific link.

I denied this, but when I thought of it later I remembered that Bob had had close working links with a Polish firm.

Then David said: 'Your husband, though, wasn't methodical. Now I'll qualify that. Home was a place to enjoy. He was precise, but *not* methodical. He put things where he wanted them to be. He knew his own filing, but woe betide anybody who tried to follow the system!'

I've already mentioned how difficult I found it to follow his filing system, after he died.

David then spoke of the great joy Bob had in coming to me.

'I feel he is contacting you, in a way, with writing. You sit alone and are suddenly becoming very impressed, and you write it down. Yet when you write it you *know* it is not you but that it's coming from a source which, your husband is telling me, is himself.'

'Yes! But I keep doubting it. That's why I asked him to confirm it through a third person.'

'Rightly.' Then David said he got the message from Bob that this would become apparent in many ways. That he would try to give me facts I know nothing about and would have to check.

'So,' he said, 'no matter how silly something may seem to you, you'll be guided as to whom to contact to find out.'

This indeed proved to be true. Over some philosophical 'talks' I had from Bob, I found I had to get guidance from his physicist friend, Peter.

David assured me that Bob would prove himself, that everything would work out all right for me and that Bob would make himself very clear. Then he made a statement that surprised me.

'I feel . . . that you're very scientific also.'

'No, I certainly am not!'

'But your husband is saying that you are! He says you are not gullible, that you'll always try to see the logical answer before you'll say that it comes from the spirit.'

How true this was, and I said so.

'I feel you're scientific and practical in thought.' Then

David repeated that he felt 'a great deal of love' between Bob and I.

This was the first time I'd been able to record a sitting on tape. It was a wonderful, stimulating experience. It gave me a feeling of 'closeness' and uplift, and now I could take that comfort home with me and have it with me for ever.

I played that tape over to many friends, one of whom was my Vicar. He was astounded to learn that David Young had never met Bob.

Half-way through the tape a strange sound interposed between the voice of David Young and my own.

'What on earth's that?' said the Vicar.

He was the first to have made any comment on this.

'Just atmospherics,' I replied.

I'd noticed the sound before myself, but had simply put it down to that.

How wrong I was!

8   Voices on tape

From that cold February day until the roses bloomed in
June, I played the tape again and again, still assuming that
it was 'atmospherics' causing that strange sound which
broke in before and after the words, 'I feel here a great
feeling of trying to communicate with you directly', in the
middle of the tape.

And then, almost by a miracle — as though Bob was
still unfolding his pattern in his own way — a leaflet fell
into my hands, enclosed in the *Service* magazine issued by
the Spiritualist Association.

It spoke of *Breakthrough*, a book by a German psy-
chologist, Dr Raudive, who after years of experiment with
a tape-recorder, claims to have picked up disembodied
voices.

What I read amazed me. Was it possible that the strange
sounds on my tape were of this order?

At once I went to get the book from the library. I was
interested but I couldn't believe such a thing could happen
to *me*!

At the time I had a German theological student staying
with me. He was anything but interested in spiritualism
— even feeling it was the work of the Devil. But he *was*
interested in the tapes. He was also very musical.

In his book, Dr Raudive mentioned that it was often difficult to appreciate the voices at first hearing, but
musically-minded people frequently found it easier to
decipher them.

I mentioned quite casually one day to the German
student that there was a strange — extraneous — sound

on the tape. At once he said if anyone could understand it, it would be his friend, Burland, who was musical and owned a tape-recorder far grander than my cheap one.

'He can run it fast or slow,' he told me. 'That would be a great help.'

That night he was going to meet his friend and I lent him the tape. I had no great feeling of excitement.

I was listening to the 10 o'clock news on television when my student burst into the sitting-room. He seemed excited and said he'd brought back my tape, but I asked him not to disturb me for a minute or two until the news was over.

Then I asked: 'Did you make anything of the tape?'

'We certainly did! Burland had to play it back three times — then it was quite clear,' he answered in his precise German accent.

He had now captured my interest, though I didn't expect anything out of the ordinary. 'What does it say?' I asked him.

Then my heart almost stopped.

'It says, "I love you, darling".' He spoke the words without emotion.

A tremor went through me. This I certainly had not expected.

I said: 'I don't believe it.'

'Please listen,' he urged. 'You will hear it yourself. It's already set up on my machine.'

I sat down opposite him, the tape-recorder between us with the tape at the spot I'd previously marked for him.

'A man very close to nature,' David is saying. And then I heard, clear as a bell, yet in a soft whisper: 'I LOVE YOU, DARLING.' Then David's words, 'I feel here this great feeling of trying to communicate with you directly.' Then my response, '. . . I don't understand.' Then again, above my own voice, louder this time, so typical of Bob, breaking up the syllables when he wanted to make himself heard: 'I LOVE YOU, DAR-LING!'

I burst into tears.

Bob's presence was real. I felt it. I was humbled, shattered. Everything tied up: his constant repetition that he

64

would 'communicate' scientifically; that emphasis of his, so typical when he wanted to attract my attention.

'You see how clear it is, once you hear it,' the student said, practically. 'And yet we didn't get it the first time.'

I couldn't sleep that night. This discovery had such wide implications. Why hadn't I recognised the words when I first played the tapes? How was it I never heard them at the interview — there had been only the sound of David's voice and my own?

It was all so wonderful — I played the tape back at that point over and over again. I *must* tell someone who'd be scientifically interested in the phenomenon and get it investigated.

I wrote a long letter to David Young telling him what had happened. I felt I had to sit with him again as soon as possible. I was able to arrange another sitting for the following week, on 4th July, 1972.

When we started the sitting, I told David Young about the discovery of the voice when I'd played the tape back at home.

On this occasion David Young seemed very tense and highly-strung, saying that my husband wasn't there and that he would take me downstairs so that I could get my fee back. I hadn't felt that upsurge of the spirit that was the usual preliminary to a good sitting.

'We can't command these things,' David said, 'but I will try.'

He switched on the tape. There was a short pause. Then he mentioned that his helper was there. To my great relief, then, he began speaking of Bob and the great force of his love.

As the sitting continued it seemed to gather spiritual strength and momentum and I began to feel the wonderful power lifting me out of myself. Then quite suddenly David said he must stop and play the tape back. This was a great disappointment to me for now the sitting had become so full of promise.

'Your husband says, "Play it back!" ' David was agitated as he reached for the tape-recorder and switched it on.

His voice was saying: 'I feel here with him that though he suffered a great deal he would try not to show it.'

'That was typical of Bob.' My voice came over softly when a faint, 'I LOVE YOU,' crept in between my voice and David's as he said:

'I sense here him saying that scientifically he is going to prove himself even more to you.'

Then came the words, 'I LOVE YOU,' much more clearly, and this startled us both. David's voice went on: '. . . and I feel here, as he is saying this to me, that he's been with you constantly.'

Here again came the words, 'I LOVE YOU,' and David's voice continuing, '. . . and he's saying here to me that he loves you very much, and he's laughing here . . . I feel here . . . a dog with him . . .'

Again that voice interjected, 'I LOVE YOU . . .'

At this point David had paused and changed the subject. 'He's laughing about your hat, by the way, because he says you used to wear some wonderful creations . . .'

Once again, 'I LOVE YOU,' was shouted in that husky voice.

'. . . And he feels that he used to like you in big hats as well.'

Here there was the sound of someone breathing deeply and, 'I LOVE YOU,' came out clearly.

Then David's voice again: '. . . A wonderful feeling of guiding you and looking after you. Oh! . . . he says the experiment is completed now. Just hold on. I'm switching off for a moment.'

We were both considerably shaken.

'That's not my voice! I must find the Secretary . . .' David leapt to his feet, leaving me alone in the room. He dashed out to find Mr Johanson, but not being able to find him he came back and sat with me again running the tape.

'Bob just wanted to prove a little thing to you,' continued David. 'He's saying it's no good trying to get too excited about things. Things may disappear for a long time but eventually may be able to come back to you. I sense here a great deal of love for you. He says he wants to show you that you are not alone. That you never will be alone and it is essential that you know it. He's laughing about the nice times you had together. But times were not always easy, were they?'

'No. He could be awkward!'

'And so could you!' replied David, and continued, 'He wants you to know that, having the scientific mind that he had on earth, he still has it and that, with many others, they are trying to help people and to show that there is a life after death. I feel here this wonderful love for you, and he says I wanted to do it for you, my dear. This is why he asked me to stop and replay.'

I asked Bob if he could put more on this tape but David replied, 'He says it's not just a question of putting more on tape. He has tried to do what he could do. I feel he is saying, Don't worry. Everything is going to be all right. God be with you. God bless you!', and the talk was at an end.

We played the tape back from the beginning where the 'extra' voice appeared, and, once again, David said he *must* find the Secretary.

When Mr Johanson joined us and listened to the tape, David said:

'There is another voice on the tape.'

The Secretary nodded. 'It's very husky.'

I needed no more convincing now that Bob had kept his promise to, 'Communicate scientifically'.

I just couldn't keep this extraordinary happening to myself. I must noise it abroad beyond the circle of my friends. I wanted to shout it from the housetops — Bob was alive and happy and trying to do everything in his power to make himself known to me; that death really *was* only the thin veil that Bob so often insisted it was. He had shown his persistence and indomitable will even on the 'other side'!

So what was my next step? I remembered that long before Bob's death I had written for some leaflets from the Churches' Fellowship for Psychical and Spiritual Studies. So I telephoned them.

They were kind and interested and put me in touch with

the Secretary of their Scientific Research Committee, Mr A.W. Rossiter, who asked me to send him the original tapes, or a copy of the 'voice'.

I daren't part with my original tapes so I sent him a copy. He said he was sure his Committee would be interested and thanked me for the dossier of events leading up to the tapes, which I had also sent him. He told me he was sending on the information to a colleague, a Mr Bearman, who was making a study of Raudive Voices.

I was delighted that someone other than myself was taking an interest in all these strange manifestations, and eventually I heard from Mr Bearman himself.

'I had hoped to get David Ellis,' he wrote, 'who is working, with a grant from a university source, on Dr Raudive's "voice phenomena", to call on you by appointment but have failed to make contact as he is in Scotland. He will be away until the end of the month. It seemed best to let you know meantime that we are desirous of following up your case, although there may be a little further delay.

'At the same time, if it should be a fact that your late husband seeks to communicate by direct voice, it might well be that Leslie Flint would be a valuable link — for Flint is outstanding.'

Perhaps it was my practical training as a journalist that was urging me on to probe and enquire and check. Certainly I was set on following up this lead from Mr Bearman.

But meanwhile enter David Ellis, a most interesting young man dedicated to the pursuit of truth.

9   Seeking proof again

It was on Monday, 14th August 1972 (sixteen months after Bob's death) that Mr Ellis came to see me.

He listened with great interest as I told him about my 'voice', but I did *not* tell him what it said. I wanted him to hear it first.

He had brought his own tape-recorder — larger and much more sensitive than mine — though he had found the voice extremely clear, he asked if he could re-record the tape for his own use.

I was only too glad to agree. At last I felt I was getting somewhere.

Mr Ellis had been given a two-year grant from Trinity College, Cambridge, and for the past two years had been attending conferences in various parts of Europe, meeting Dr Raudive and other scientists and testing out this new phenomenon.

At the same time, he was writing and distributing a series of Reports on his work (later published as *The Mediumship of the Tape Recorder*) and he included me in the last part of his Report No. 19. As he was a scientist, his statements were very guarded, but they make interesting reading. Here is an extract:

'I visited Victoria Stevenson at her home on 14th August, and listened to, and copied, selections of tape-recordings of the sittings which she had had with the medium, Mr David Young. On each were audible extra words, not apparently spoken by the medium but nevertheless reinforcing what he was saying. About half-way through the first sitting (which lasted some forty-five minutes) a simple message was uttered twice, in a hoarse whisper, and during the second (which was very short) another very simple message occurred no less than six times, sometimes clearly and sometimes indistinctly.

'The recordings were made on a cheap cassette recorder which was operated by Mr Young, who held the (not very sensitive) microphone in his hand as he was talking. Although he could possibly have uttered the "messages" himself — they occur between his words and could have been voiced as he was taking a breath — it is debatable whether he could have done so, particularly on the second occasion, without Victoria Stevenson noticing, as she was sitting only a few feet away from him. Moreover, the extreme agitation which he showed on playing back the tape of the second sitting, and hearing the extra voice on it is hardly consistent with deliberate fraud.

'If the voice effects were genuine, they show several interesting features, perhaps the most important being their relative clarity . . . and the evidence of purpose shown by their repetition. It is interesting to note that Victoria Stevenson's husband, through Mr Young, said he was trying to communicate with her directly and mentioned direct voice. The final message of the second sitting was, "he says . . . the experiment is completed now."

'It was obvious that the next step in the study was to see if the voice effects could be repeated under more controlled conditions, so a further sitting was arranged for Victoria Stevenson with Mr Young, at which I was able to be present, record the proceedings on my own machine (with the microphone at some distance from the medium) and listen carefully for any extra voices. However, although the results were otherwise very satisfactory, no such voices could be heard on the recordings.

'Victoria Stevenson's husband had been a scientist and, finding a fellow scientist in myself, spent most of the session talking to me.'

As can be imagined this sitting was a great disappointment to me. Bob didn't address me but, as David Ellis has reported, carried on a philosophical talk with him. It was much too deep for me to follow, though a physicist friend, on reading the transcript of the tape later, considered it evocative and relevant to our research on voices.

All through the sitting David Young seemed to be wrestling with unfamiliar phrases as though translating from a foreign language! Obviously it was difficult and trying for him — the sitting lasted nearly an hour.

At one point when David Ellis urged him to go on, he said:

'I'll try — but I think, since he was a scientist on earth, he should have another scientist to deal with him — one gifted with mediumship.'

The message then came through David Young from Bob:

'Not everyone understands radar. Neither do they understand frequency or what it is . . .'

To show what David Young was up against, and how incomprehensible the conversation was to me, I quote what follows next on the tape:

'. . . They understand an impulse or they can do an analysis of an impulse but do not necessarily know that the frequency and the impulse are two different things. And yet all life is made up of frequencies. If you like to take an atom and take it down, we have frequencies.

'It doesn't just come through a channel . . . making another person hear you. It's the same thing as putting a frequency on a tape. There's no difference in it at all. It seems to be serving the same sort of purpose . . . Of course anagrams are easy to solve when you've got space to fit in the words. The anagram of life can never be solved because it is continuous.'

In the following months David Ellis often joined Bob's friend, Peter, and myself for fireside chats on a Saturday evening. Bob had suggested this in his talk with David Young.

Sometimes with soft background music, sometimes without, we'd sit quietly talking, with the tape running — but without result, except that Peter, being psychic as

I've said before, often said he felt Bob's presence. On one occasion he said Bob was holding up a Dew-Point Hygrometer (meaningless to me!), this proving his identity to them both.

One evening, however, in November, David let his tape run on for about an hour but had no time to play it back just then. He said he would do so at his leisure, later in the week.

The following Saturday, Peter and I were sitting together when the telephone rang. It was David Ellis phoning from Epping.

'I've just played the tape back,' he said excitedly, 'and I've got "extras"! Can I play them to you over the telephone?'

Peter said: 'Useless. We'd never hear them.'

'Then I'll come over right away,' said David.

This worried me as it was already eight o'clock and it meant an hour's journey each way for him. He brushed that aside and duly arrived.

He set up his tape-recorder and we all three sat down to listen.

We heard a sound like, 'ut, ut, ut', as though someone were hesitating between words. Then: 'Bob,' and finally what sounded like, 'Maggot'. But that seemed ridiculous.

'Would it be "agate"?' Peter asked, turning to me. 'Does that make sense to you?'

'No,' I said.

Then as we replayed the tape again and again I was sure it must be 'Robert,' — Bob's full name.

They weren't startling, these 'extras', but interesting in that a third voice had appeared on tape, at a carefully supervised sitting. I felt convinced that Bob was keeping his promise to David Ellis that he would try to appear on tape without a medium.

Mr Ellis explains in his Report No. 20 how he played back many of his collected 'voices' to eight members of the Cambridge University Society for Psychical Research. I quote:

'The participants wrote down their interpretations, usually while the tape was being played. On rare occasions comments were made, but the influence of these on other listeners' interpretations is not thought to have been very great. (They provoked argument rather than agreement.)'

The listeners had not been told, of course, what David Ellis and I thought was on the tape. Although their interpretations varied a little, the agreement was close enough for Mr Ellis to sum up (for one set of voices):

'A voice whispers, "I love you," clearly, at least once. The speaker is very near to the microphone.'

And about the other set:

'A voice says "I love you, darling," twice, fairly clearly.' His report goes on:

'Victoria Stevenson seems to be a very successful sitter and had several good sittings with London mediums before those with Mr David Young, during which the extras occurred. Copies of extras were used in Listening Test I, and their clarity demonstrated.

'Another feature worthy of note was the way the second, "I love you, darling," was uttered: it was very characteristic of the slow, deliberate way in which her husband, in a final attempt to make himself heard, used to shout to his wife from upstairs.

'. . . Her husband's scientific colleague and friend joined us for further experimental recordings. He suggested that we try table-tilting and we were soon able to get messages from Bob in this way.

'Both through the table and through his wife, Bob said that he would do his best to put his voice on the tape, and claimed success for his earlier efforts (with David Young, myself and Victoria Stevenson). We made a number of recordings during the table-tilting, sitting quietly, with her holding the microphone but we listened in vain for any extras.'

10   Direct voices

The first sitting I had with Mr Leslie Flint, the famous
Direct Voice medium, was on 2nd June 1972. He is so
much sought after by people from all over the world that I
had to make the appointment months in advance.

He had, as I've mentioned, been recommended to me
but I had no idea what to expect.

Seven of us gathered in his sitting-room, settled on easy
chairs and settees, and one couple even sat on the floor at
Mr Flint's feet with their tape-recorders. (This I discovered
was a key position. With my little cheap machine, and sitting at the other end of the room, I wasn't able to record all
of the conversation.)

Mr Flint's 'intermediary' with the spirit world is Micky,
a little Cockney boy who, I learned, used to sell news-
papers outside Camden Town underground station and
was killed in a street accident after the First World War.

The lights were turned out and we all sat in complete
darkness. Mr Flint gave the date of the sitting and introduced himself, saying that no medium could guarantee
results. We might, he said, sit there for an hour with nothing happening. There was nothing one could do about it.
The important thing was to be natural. A wrong attitude
towards the other side, or tenseness and anxiety would be
a barrier.

'In other words,' said Mr Flint, 'if somebody comes and
calls you by name or gives an indication of who the person
is, for heaven's sake speak up. This is most important. It's
like the telephone: if you don't answer it you won't get
anywhere.

'The voices vary,' he went on. 'Sometimes they're loud, distinct, clear, with a personality and characteristics. At other times they don't sound a scrap like the person they are. It's one of those things! One doesn't know what the answers will be . . . but even if you don't recognise the voice let it realise you respond. It's not so much the *sound* of the voice but what it says that really is important, I think.'

He went on to say he didn't go into trances. 'It would be very unusual if I do. I'm quite normal, and if I think it necessary to talk to the voices I will, but I prefer to keep out of the picture.'

He stressed that he didn't want to intrude into what was *our* sitting and whether it was a success or failure would depend on our response.

'Don't concentrate on any one person. It inhibits, in some strange way. It's quite natural to do this but I think it's a big mistake. Try to remember, too, that if you're seeking evidence of survival, the best evidence is from people you least expect, even if you have to check up afterwards. We don't have any hymn-singing. We don't have any prayers.'

If anyone for any reason, he told us, was not satisfied with the sitting he didn't want a fee.

'I don't want anyone to walk out of my flat unless they're satisfied . . . I like to feel my work stands the test. I'm prepared to answer any questions.'

Then he said: 'What about the lady on the couch?' (This was me.) 'Do you want to ask anything?'

I said I was quite happy.

For a short while there was general talk about the Raudive Voices. I told them my own story which seemed to interest everyone. It was strange talking to unseen people in total darkness.

And then, quite suddenly, the voice of Micky, Mr Flint's spirit-helper, broke into our conversation and everyone fell silent.

He seemed to go round the gathering, recognising old friends, until he came to the gentleman sitting next to me.

In a strong Cockney voice Micky asked him whether I was with him. Receiving a negative answer he then turned his attention to me. He said my husband was there.

'He is? I'm delighted!'

The room had become very still and I could almost hear my heart-beats.

'He knew you were coming this afternoon,' Micky said, 'and . . . I don't know what he means by it . . . changing your route . . . but he says you weren't quite sure whether that was the right way.'

'You're quite right,' I said. Mr Flint's flat is in a part of London I didn't know well.

'And you couldn't quite make up your mind and he had to lead you because he didn't want you to get lost!'

I said my husband did a lot of leading.

'He says he's often around you and he sort of guides you and tries to help you in various ways.'

'I think he does. I *know* he does!'

'By the way,' Micky said, 'you're wearing something belonging to him.'

There was a soft muttering as though Micky was conversing with someone behind the scenes.

'Can he speak to me himself?' I was so thrilled that I'd quite forgotten the unseen listeners.

'I hope so, love,' Micky answered, 'but give me a breather!' and then turned his attention to the lady sitting next to me. 'Are you Bobby?' he asked.

She said she was not.

'That's funny,' said Micky. 'Someone here is talking about Bobby. Is there someone here called Bobby?'

There was a short silence and a whispering again between Micky and someone else. Then silence. Presently Mr Flint said:

'There was one lady who couldn't come, Micky.'

Another silence. Then I said, 'My husband's name was Bob, Micky.'

'I don't know,' he said. 'There's a bloke here who keeps pushing me and he's laughing all over his face, and he says "You tell her"; and he keeps on about Bobby.'

'Bob! His name's Bob,' I cried excitedly. 'He's a bit forceful, isn't he?'

'He's a strong personality,' Micky declared. 'He's a bit too much for me, missus! Have you got him well-trained?' This amused the unseen audience.

'I think he trained *me*!' I laughed.

There was a further silence lasting a few seconds and then . . . Bob himself came through. It didn't sound like Bob's voice — and I told him so. He sounded so grand.

'That's because I'm having to speak through this confounded box!' he said. He sounded commanding and emphatic, and I could hear clearly what he was saying.

He spoke about the voices on tape, that he was still trying to repeat his 'performance' and asked me, when alone, to sit with the tape running. He talked of our home and put personal questions. He spoke with emphasis and humour, and kept the invisible audience in fits of laughter. Then quite suddenly a voice called across:

'Doris! Doris!'

This is my first name, the one my family always called me by.

'This is Mother!' It was a light, bright, feminine voice. I recognised it at once as Mother's.

'Darling!' I cried. 'I'd forgotten *you*!'

I meant, of course, that concentrating so hard on Bob I'd forgotten my beloved mother for whom I'd grieved so much, until that day I sat with Mr Redmond.

'You've got a short memory!' She laughed — just as she would have done on earth. 'I've come with Bob. I'll leave you with him.'

Once again Bob came through and our talk must have lasted for at least half-an-hour. Then another voice cut in and Bob faded out.

I had had, of course, to run the tapes in total darkness, and it was unfortunate that my microphone did not pick up his questions and answers very clearly. Also the tape ran out half-way through the sitting.

But in spite of this it was a marvellous sitting and afterwards people crowded around me and congratulated me on, 'having such a scientific husband.' I did feel a little guilty, though, at having stolen the limelight, leaving other sitters with only a few brief messages — and some none at all.

David Ellis was so interested when he heard of my sitting and Bob's assertion that he was still trying to get through on tape, that he agreed to join me at my next sitting with Mr Flint. But this didn't take place until a year later, on 8th May 1973.

As Leslie Flint had predicted — that no two sittings were alike — this second one was quite different from the first. For one thing, there were ten sitters, instead of the usual seven or eight.

Again the medium said that nothing could be guaranteed. We then chatted among ourselves waiting for Micky's voice. It was a long wait — just about an hour.

Mr Flint repeated that some sittings were good, others abortive. No one knew the reason why — it could be atmospherics, or the attitude of the sitters.

This medium has a far-flung audience. On this occasion two women had come down specially from Manchester, others came from South Africa and Australia.

Once or twice during a lull in the conversation Mr Flint called, 'Micky!' Then out of the darkness came a very faint whispered, 'David.'

'What does he say? I can't hear, Micky,' Mr Flint called.

Then came another, 'David!' and David Ellis replied.

'I know you. You're David Ellis,' came from Micky, who then told him he had a lot of power. 'Did you come with that lady, Vic?'

I pricked up my ears!

'Are you with Vicky?' persisted the little Cockney voice. 'It's one of the names people call you, but it's not the name commonly used.'

This seemed to me remarkable evidence: my Christian names are Doris Victoria, the first used by my family, and the second I use as my pen-name. I replied:

'Quite right, Micky. How did you know?'

'Because your Mum's telling me.'

'My mother!' I'd been thinking only of Bob.

'Don't be so surprised, girl. She's here!'

For the next little while Micky turned his attention to David Ellis, talked about his present work and what a strong power of mediumship he had. Then out of the blue Micky mentioned my name again.

'Have you known this Vic long? I like her. She's a nice lady. Her mother's very close to her.'

I laughed. 'And you're a nice boy, Micky!'

'I don't know about that, girl. I do my job. Sit. Hold tight. I'll be back.'

There seemed to be some confusion for Micky was whispering, 'What about that other lot? I don't know them. They sit in a circle.'

This may have referred to two other friends of mine who were interested in my 'voice'. They were sitting on the other side of the room. The whispered conversation ended with, 'Oh, shut up!' Then, 'Victoria!' came over the air, very faintly.

'Victoria!' A soft feminine voice whispered this a second time. 'I'm not sure whether you can hear what I'm saying. *Can* you hear me? It's Mother.'

'But — you never called me by my second name before!'

'I know.' The voice was audible, but faint. 'But I thought today I would, because it's not usual for you to use that name. But the little boy seems to have cottoned on to the idea!'

'It doesn't sound quite like your voice, darling,' I replied, 'but it's lovely to hear you. Is Bob with you?'

'Yes. It's this box, I suppose. I don't understand much about it. All I know is that I could come and speak through — this box business — and I hope you can hear what I'm saying!'

She said Bob was with her — and Charles.

'I don't know Charles.' Whereupon Micky's chirpy voice told me she had several people with her, my father among them.

'In fact,' he said, 'there's a little crowd with your Mum.

79

They've all come to support her, and there was a Charles on your father's side of the family. Don't worry — some of your relations have been here for donkey's years!'

He broke off. Then suddenly: 'D'you know the name of P . . .' mentioning my married name. 'Your husband's here and he says, Tell her that P . . . is here.'

At first I wondered why Bob should use his surname. Then it struck me: David Ellis, who'd never known him personally, and a business associate of Bob's were also present. As though reading my thoughts, Micky explained:

'He's got a special reason for giving his surname. He wouldn't give his Christian name. He's saying, 'You tell her that P . . . is here and — hold on! there's a lady he knows here besides yourself. He says you brought her with you, and that David bloke." '

Once more I was struck by the accuracy of the messages. There were a few more about a change around the house, and a lady, 'pushing herself in', saying, 'I'm Nell.' (I'd recently lost a dear friend of that name.)

There was more whispering, 'back-stage', as though Micky were having trouble marshalling his speakers. Then:

'No! I don't want anyone else. I want her husband.'

Then a scarcely audible voice: 'You say who I am . . . Bob.'

I felt excited. 'Bob!' I shouted. 'I can't hear you very well, dear.'

A voice came through that I couldn't recognise as Bob's but it was firm and commanding. 'I'm sorry. I'm shouting and trying to speak as loudly as I can.'

I couldn't help laughing. 'You sound like a very enfeebled old gentleman — and that you're certainly not!'

'I know I'm not,' said the faint voice, 'but don't blame me, blame this thing I have to speak through. Can you hear me?'

I told him I could.

'I'm not sure I can manage to speak as loudly as I'd like, but I'll try — to let you know I'm here. I'm with your mother and father. We're all here together. I've met so many people here — relations and friends of yours and mine. Can you hear me?'

Again I told him, yes. He mentioned music and I asked him if it helped when we played it at home.

'That's what I mean. I try my utmost to draw near to you, and I must say I find music's a great help. Continue the circle.' Here I felt he was referring to the times David Ellis and I sat together at home. 'I'm hoping eventually we shall be able to manifest and communicate. There's so much we want to do.'

'Who do you want me to have in the circle?'

Bob said he must leave that to me, but he'd like the opportunity of making contact at home.

There was another long pause. Then Micky chipped in: 'I think he's terribly excited and rather tensed up.' Then, as though he were giving instructions to the participants on the other side, 'Hold on!'

Bob's voice came through again. 'David . . . Mr Ellis? I'm glad to think you've joined the circle.'

Then Micky again:

'I think he's anxious for that Mr Ellis to be linked up with your circle. I told you at the beginning there's a lot of power with that young lad.'

He went on to say that Bob was sending his love to my sister and that he was finding it a little difficult to contact today. 'I don't know why,' he said. Then he spoke of Lulu, a mutual friend of Bob's and mine, and told me there were crowds of people there for me, apart from Bob and my parents.

He broke off abruptly and seemed to be talking to those 'offstage' again.

There was another long pause and we waited silently in the darkness. Mr Flint called Micky and suggested he try someone else. But still we waited. Then the name, 'Doris', repeated several times, floated on the air.

As I'd been the only one to receive a message, apart from David Ellis, I hesitated to claim attention. But the voice kept on calling, 'Doris!' and as no one replied, I said: 'That's me!'

'Can you hear me, Doris?' This time the voice was much stronger.

I said: 'Is that you, Bob?'

'Of course it is! I was so amused at Mother calling you Victoria. We've just been having a little chat about it and I asked her whatever made her call you that. She said, "Well, I thought it would be interesting to let her know I hadn't forgotten her second name." So I said: "Please don't do it again. I've never liked the name!" '

'You certainly never called me that in your life!'

'Well, I thought I'd get that sorted out. I didn't intend to call you Victoria. I just wanted to call you Doris — *my* Doris!'

Then the voice gaining tremendous strength went on:

'That young lad there. I do hope he'll sit in the circle. I do want him because I think he'd make a good medium . . . I think he might be a great help to a lot of people eventually.'

'You're remarkably clear now, Bob,' I said.

'Thank the Lord for that!' interrupted Micky.

I laughed. 'Thank *you*, Micky.'

'Well, that's my job. But you have to depend on conditions. They vary so — fluctuating all the time from good, bad to indifferent. No sitting's ever alike. Vibrations change. It's difficult to make people understand. I do my bit because I'm used to it, but some of the people find great difficulty . . . I can *assert* myself and get over, but some can't — poor things!'

He then switched to the friends of mine sitting across the room, and linked them with me. But Bob was heard no more.

Friends have asked me, 'Why sit in darkness?' and, 'What do the "voices" mean when they mention they have to use a "box"?' I can only say that I was so amazed at the sittings and it was not until this book was about to be published that I put the question to Mr Flint, who told me that all Physical Mediums work in darkness as power and energy are drawn from the body of the medium and exude, as ectoplasm, a living substance which forms the artificial voice box. Sometimes they are recognisable, sometimes not.

11 Daybreak

Even now I was not content, in spite of the close contact with Bob that had been building up. Was it really just a series of extraordinary coincidences?

The inspirational talks *should* have satisfied me; I'd had assurance of comradeship through those early mediums; I'd had the 'voice' on tape. Why was my mind not at rest, my quest ended?

Without any effort on my part there had been other odd incidents too. One of these was on my visit to our little Spiritualist Church. I was introduced there to the late Mrs Vigurs, the Honorary Vice-President, who'd been connected with the movement for years. I had never met her before, nor even heard of her.

I was talking to someone else when she broke into our conversation with:

'Your husband! What a tremendously strong personality! It's so strange, he seems to keep kicking up the carpet with his right foot, bending his knees as though stumbling and about to fall.'

To say I was astonished would be to put it mildly. As I've already mentioned, Bob had lost a leg and often used to catch a loose mat with his artificial foot.

'He's trying to identify himself,' she said. 'I'm not a medium, but I sometimes get these glimpses of things.'

I went on with my conversation, but Mrs Vigurs again broke in with:

'This husband of yours! He's laughing all over his face! Have you something in your kitchen which goes "Fizz" and makes a noise?'

I couldn't think of anything for the moment. Then she suggested:

'Have you a pressure-cooker? It looks as if he's holding one and letting the steam out, as a joke.'

I'd always been afraid of the things, but I remembered that one day — much against my will! — Bob brought one home. It always amused him to see me trying to cope with it, until I finally got used to it.

Other incidents cropped up, such as the time a friend of mine, interested in spiritualism, came to stay with me. She was most impressed by a recording of Lillian Stubley's tape (which I refer to later). As a result my friend went to buy herself a tape-recorder so that she could take a recording home with her.

When a month later I received a Christmas card from her it contained a note telling me she had been to the Bath Spiritualist Church in Bournemouth, where the late Jordan Gill (another well-known medium, of whom more later) was demonstrating at short notice.

Out of all the crowds in the church, he picked my friend and asked her if the name 'Doris' meant anything to her. (Most of my friends know me by this name.) He said I lived not in the country but, 'off the beaten track,' which is true enough as my house is outside the town, down a lane.

We both thought this remarkable.

Another rather unusual incident occurred. *Woman's Own* had published an article of mine about my voices on tape. A photo of the medium, David Young, and myself illustrated the text. One day a woman in Durham telephoned the Features Editor of the magazine to say that she could clearly see the face of a man behind my left shoulder, in the photograph. She thought at first this must be a printer's error, so bought a second copy — only to find the face still there!

I got in touch with this reader by telephone and she described the face as without wrinkles and with a broad forehead (typical of Bob), and said she could identify it if I sent a group photo.

I sent two snapshots of Bob surrounded by friends of his

own age. Three of them were very different, but one closely resembled him. In fact they might have been brothers — full faces, receding hair, firm mouths.

The reader telephoned me to say she was having difficulty, because two figures in the photograph were so much alike. She marked Bob and the friend who was so like him!

Despite these new, sometimes trifling adventures into the Realm of Spirit, I was still driven forward by an even stonger urge to find more proof, more confirmation from a third party and a yearning for the miracle of the voices to appear on another tape.

While all these 'happenings' were taking place, and those others mentioned in previous chapters, I sat at intervals over a period of two years with some half-dozen London mediums.

All confirmed Bob's nearness and his efforts to communicate, but of them all the late Jordan Gill and Lillian Stubley were the most outstanding.

I had not met either of them before, yet on that bleak December day nearly two years after Bob's death, Jordan Gill gave a perfect picture of Bob, as he saw him standing beside me.

'I don't consider him old,' he began. 'There were years of experience there, if you can understand me, but there was no age in the man. I like him. He's very close to you at the moment. I'd say he was about 5 foot 10 inches.'

When I checked Bob's passport later I found his height given as 5 foot 9 inches.

Jordan went on: 'He had very good shoulders, well-built, well-proportioned, with rather an intellectual forehead. He had a very good nose, broadening a little at the base. The lips are a little full, but not sensuous — sensitive rather. The jaw is quite firm, almost square.'

I couldn't have described him so well myself.

'But what I want to say is, when he smiles his face lights up! But there's also something wise that appeals to me — that is, he's a man of knowledge.'

'He was,' I said.

'Is!' Mr Gill replied with emphasis. 'Forgive me pointing

this out — he *is* a man of knowledge, not *was*! You could listen to him. If he was interested he was a conversationalist. If he wasn't — then he couldn't suffer fools lightly . . . he was used to people and the handling of people. He was often called on to take responsibility in many ways. I'd say, literally, he used himself up and in the end passed quickly. It was something of a shock to you when the time came.'

Once again a medium had got the measure of Bob's character and personality.

He now went on to say that my own life was not without purpose, that my husband would accompany me every step of the way . . . that until I 'crossed the bridge' to join him we should often meet across the bridge, half-way — meaning of course that he was keeping in touch with me.

'You are a journalist and should write a book. You will have spiritual guidance.'

I told him I was indeed thinking of doing this, to which he replied that unless I did so, 'the purpose would be lost.'

'Don't keep your ideas in your mind for too long. Try and set them down and the inspiration will flow.'

One sunny September afternoon the following year I sat with Lillian Stubley, who at once asked if I had anything to do with books or writing. This surprised me.

She spoke of a man, very close to me, holding up a wedding ring, and continued, 'This gentleman keeps showing me books, putting them on the table. It seems to me as I look at one . . . there is something — half-way through.'

This was certainly true since I was in the midst of writing this very book!

She said something was holding me up — that I was waiting for spiritual guidance, but the time was now right for me to go ahead.

'This gentleman is walking so close to you. Closer than hands or feet or breathing. He's saying, "Don't worry! In time you'll be able to write what's in your mind." '

Then she spoke, as so many other mediums had, of Bob's quick passing, 'There was no time to say goodbye. The blood rushed to his head, only for a moment, then he passed very quickly.

'. . . This husband of yours,' she went on, '. . . was moved out of your life so quickly — as though you crossed the desert without hope, almost without feeling, yet . . . it's almost like a miracle! As swiftly as he'd gone out of it, he came back into it, as though you walked with him.

'He's talked with you, he has guided you spiritually and materially, just as though in some way he's always been with you. You know this is true: that you've been together, that just a thin veil separates you.

'It seems as if when he's walked with you, he's not only opened the doors of your conscious mind but he's filled it with spiritual thoughts, has helped you in some way not only to accept for yourself this realisation of life after death, but in a way has used you as a channel by which you could reach the world in general — or those of us who are open to receive it — to tell us more of these truths.'

Then she said: 'I don't know whether this is shown in your writing, or whether it's your personality that is passing it on to others. But I do feel this is his intention.'

Then the medium said she heard the name Bob — or Robert — and that she felt he was the one who was talking, telling me, 'in some way — I don't know what it is — that you have a decision to make . . . As though you were reaching a turning-point; he's saying "All right, darling, I'm still in command." '

Then she asked if Bob was my husband and told me he was saying he was right behind me, helping to steer me.

'There seem to be times when you're wondering whether you're doing right, as though you're half-way through something that's being written, and *he's* working at it; that the main links will be given to you through his love and through those who are helping you.

'No matter how or when or where your life works out, he says he'll always follow every avenue of it, in varying experiments or moves. Live each day knowing he is with you and making decisions with you . . . This husband of yours is a very remarkable spirit!'

'I've been told this before,' I said.

'Yes! But he's remarkable because of the love you shared, and the link you've kept with him. But — I do feel that you have — or he's been trying to put through — a psychic drawing . . . It's strange, but I just feel there *will* be something that will be put through the spirit.'

I wondered if this had to do with the strange voice on tape — which of course she could know nothing about.

She asked then: 'Have you heard your husband speak to you?'

I told her I had sat with Leslie Flint.

'You see. That's what I felt! Direct voice! And yet — I feel you must have heard him yourself — almost as though he was telling you to do things, or guiding you to make decisions.'

I felt this was certainly true, and I asked if she meant proving his existence.

'Oh yes! I feel he *has* proved it to you in many ways.'

Suddenly she said: 'Surrey! Does Surrey mean anything to you?'

'Why, yes! Surrey is where I live.'

'Your husband is taking me there. He's saying — I don't know why — "Well, darling. It's just the same as when we were together."

'It's strange — but there's such a relationship between you two that it's almost as though — he isn't where he is. But of course he isn't! He's here in the room with us. He's here with you!'

'I've often said,' I told her, ' "I wish you'd let me see you!" '

'Oh, but you will! May I suggest that you don't strain so much . . . Just say, "Bob, I know when it's right for *you*, then I'll see you." You *must* release them! You have to conform to the law. It's like electricity. When you want to get light you have to press the switch connecting the wire to the light.'

I was beginning to understand.

'In the same way,' she continued, 'if we are concentrating and transmitting our own energy by thought, we fill our own mind so that nothing can get through. Just release it. Don't keep using *your* mental powers.'

She said we must let them manipulate the power and the law. They're at different vibrations from ours.

'Just say, "I don't know how you go on over there, but I'm sure *you* do. And when you're ready I'll be there." '

I didn't record the end of this remarkable sitting because the tape ran out, but I'd received such comfort and uplift from it. I was so conscious of Bob's continual presence and power.

No day in our earthly life is complete and self-contained — with its hangover from yesterday intermingled with plans for the future. So, it seems, I am unable in my quest for truth to draw a line and say, 'I have reached the end.'

12   More practical help

Over the years since Bob left me physically, I've almost grown used to his overshadowing, spiritual presence. Sometimes it is so strong I feel I could reach out and touch him.

There are other times, though, when I allow depression to get a stranglehold on me, when he seems unable to get through to me. Not surprising, really, since as I've recorded he has told me more than once, in our inspirational talks, that my deep grief is a barrier he's unable to cross. At these times he has begged me to make the effort, to act as though he is always beside me.

Now I find myself naturally turning to him in all sorts of small panics and anxieties, and he seldom fails me.

It can hardly be coincidence when the problem concerns mechanical things, which to me are a closed book! Bob always knew this — if ever he found me with a screwdriver or other tool in my hand he'd beg me to put it down and let him do the job!

I am not a keen driver and never have been. I use the car for the very practical reason that my house is isolated and far from the town. I'd be static without some means of transport. But as for knowing anything about the workings of a car, my mind's a blank.

Imagine then my horror one day, when I'd come back from a short trip, to find, as I thought, the garage on fire, smoke billowing out.

I leapt out — to find the smoke was actually steam pouring from my car.

Panic!

I'd never so much as raised the bonnet — I always leave the mechanics at the garage to attend to anything to do with the car. So what was I to do now?

Quite unexpectedly calm settled on me. A clear message came into my mind.

'Open the bonnet.' But the catch was so stiff I couldn't budge it — and still the steam came gushing out!

Without more ado — as though someone else was taking over — I went into the kitchen, fetched a piece of string and slipped it under the catch, pulled — and the catch was released. Splendid!

I seemed to be filled with a strong, quiet power. I fixed open the bonnet and let the engine steam.

As if Bob were controlling my brain the thought came: 'Now go and sit down for half-an-hour and watch the cricket. Let it cool.'

All panic vanished as though he were there in person.

I spent an enjoyable interlude watching cricket on television and went back to the car. Actually I was afraid to touch it — surely everything inside would be burned and cracked?

'Take off the radiator cap,' was the next mental message. This I'd never done in my life before, but I *had* seen the garage workers do it.

'Now fill it up,' came next.

I followed instructions, though how was I to know there mightn't be a hole in the radiator?

'Now drive slowly to the garage,' was the next inspired order.

I wondered about this. Could I be sure it wouldn't break down en route? However, all went well.

When I took the car to the garage and told my story to the lad at the pumps, he looked underneath and found a leaking radiator.

'I'll soon fix that.' He poured in some solution or other and I drove home happy.

But I hadn't finished with my car problems. I still felt worried and restless that evening. Was the car *really* all right?

Then came quite clearly into my mind: 'Get Dave to look at it.'

Dave was a motor engineer who had always serviced Bob's car. So I rang him the next morning.

'Your rad's all right,' he said after examining the car. 'But there's a leak somewhere. I think the bottom-hose has perished. I'll have a look.'

Of course he was right. The extra expense of replacing the bottom-hose was a nuisance, but I was relieved that my 'wild imagination' had been proved right.

It was as if, sometimes, I was relaxing in Bob's arms.

There were other simpler things, too, like the day I lost my car-keys (who hasn't!). Anyone living alone will know the frustration of having no one at hand to advise or discuss things with.

I had just come back from a happy day with my sister. It was half past nine in the evening. I closed the garage, locked the door and went into the house, putting my handbag on the kitchen table as I passed through.

Normally I fling my car-keys beside it, but when I came back to fetch my bag, they were not there.

Where could I have put them? I'd only been through to the sitting-room, but they certainly were not there. Neither were they in my bag. I began to panic. All sorts of wild thoughts went through my mind. Had I left them at my sister's? How ridiculous — I couldn't have driven home if I had!

I went round the house. I looked in every nook and cranny. I looked in coat pockets.

And then, like a cool breeze fanning me: 'Stop the panic! Go out to the car,' came clearly into my mind.

It was dark now, but I went to unlock the garage and switched on the light. I expected to find the keys in the lock. But no, they weren't there.

I locked up everything again and went back to the house after the abortive trip. But I couldn't rest. Still the thought kept nagging me, 'Go out to the car!'

So out I went again and searched. Nothing!

Where on earth were they? Another intensive search —

still to no effect. This exercise had now taken an hour, but I couldn't go to bed until I'd found the keys.

With the persistent directive still ringing in my head, out I went again. This time I took a torch with me, shining it in front of me as I crossed the courtyard.

On the paving-stones in front of the garage lay my keys. What relief!

At times like these it is as if Bob sighs and says: 'At last I've made it. *At last* you understand!'

In July that year I had been told by a specialist that I should have a minor operation on my ear. It was to be done in London, but there were weeks of delay and when it came to the point I funked it! My doctor then suggested a local specialist and this made things much easier for me, as he said I could have the operation the very next day.

Unfortunately this was the 39th anniversary of our wedding and four months before I'd booked a sitting with a well-known medium as a special treat for the occasion. I had had sittings with this medium for two years, always with wonderful results.

I hated to cancel the appointment, for it might be months before I could get another. But I had to make up my mind right away, so I agreed to the operation, with much regret, and cancelled the sitting.

That evening I rang my sister to tell her of my decision, and also of my disappointment over the sitting, which now had been postponed until November.

The following day, to my surprise, my sister telephoned at eleven in the morning.

'You know I don't usually ring at this expensive time,' she said. (She is strictly practical, always to the point — and a rock to lean on.) 'But — this sounds strange and I'd never mention it to anyone else — early this morning I woke up and it was just as though Bob was speaking to me. He said, "Tell Doris not to be disappointed about cancelling the sitting. It's so much more important to get her ear done." I just felt, dear, I had to tell you and that it would relieve your mind.'

Imagine my delight at such an unexpected communication from my down-to-earth sister. I felt Bob was very near me in my trouble.

That evening I felt particularly lonely — with our anniversary in my mind — so I decided on early-to-bed with a book. I went to select one, but nothing seemed to appeal.

Then the idea came to me to take one of my tapes and play it back in bed — a thing I hadn't done for years. So I went to choose one. Which should it be?

I thought of the medium, Mrs Ivy Scott, with whom I should have had the sitting that day. I'd had one with her a while back but could not remember the details.

I chose this early tape, settled in bed comfortably, switched off the light and began playing it back. The soothing voice relaxed me.

She began: 'You have so many spirit friends around you. They are like a gathering . . . You have a husband in the spirit world and he was the first to arrive . . . I want to give you from your husband a bouquet of deep red velvety roses. He tells me he is closer to you now than he's ever been. He says — and he has a wonderful sense of humour — to tell you the longer he's here, the younger he looks, and when you meet him the years that have passed will fall away from you and you will look to him the same number of years that he looks to you, so that he will be young and in his prime, and so will you — because it is all a mental approach to life.'

She spoke of Bob, my mother and father and, as I'd been told so often before, that I was psychic. She also referred to his sudden passing, as had so many others.

'When he first came over here he kept saying, "Why me? Why *me*? There are all the unwanted, the aged, the cripples. It just didn't make sense. But when I calmed down a little, and they told me that if I'd continued breathing I should have been a vegetable, I did say, well, God works in a mysterious way. It takes a little understanding." Now he's quite content about it.'

Then she told me: 'He says, "My wife often wonders whether I am happy. Tell her there are so many types of happiness. I am now a well man, vigorous and energetic.

I'm in a world where I can explore and learn, and in that way I'm happy because I am fulfilled. But tell my wife I shall not be complete until she joins me. It's quite possible that we can progress away from the earth, but at the same time I am with her. However long I have to wait for her I shall be here when she comes over. She will know when she's leaving the earth because, even before she draws her last breath she will see me waiting for her, and I will show her the way".'

The medium broke off, then asked me if I'd had a word with Bob to say I was coming here today, and I told her I had.

'Because he says he was prepared for you today. He walked down the road with you. You live in a house?'

'Yes.'

'I keep seeing a house and a beautiful blue net over it. Lovely! It's a spiritual thing. Like a cloak of protection around the home. And I feel that nothing untoward which could disturb you could happen there. I feel it is so protected by your spirit friends, your loved ones and your helpers. They are so strongly there with you. When you sit quietly they are close to you.'

'I feel my husband is.'

'Yes! And when you're quiet he tries to keep you so . . . Have you a lawn at the back of your house? I see you sitting on a lawn and your husband promenading up and down.'

Towards the end of this very happy sitting, to my astonishment the medium said: 'Is there an anniversary around now? July?'

'Yes! It was our wedding anniversary.'

'I asked your husband just now,' she told me, 'when he placed those red roses in your lap and he said, "Tell my wife they're for the anniversary . . ." '

In the quiet, twilit bedroom I sat bolt upright. I felt Bob was with me, talking to me.

How extraordinary! Why on that particular evening did I feel the urge to play back a tape when usually I read in bed? And why, out of all the recordings should I have chosen the only one that mentions our anniversary?

13 Dreaming

Dreams have been a mystery to man since the beginning of time. Are they prophetic, as in the Bible? Do they foretell the future, as some people claim, or do we leave our body and wander on other planes?

The medium, Mrs Ivy Scott had told me: 'When you are in your sleep state you travel a great deal and meet your husband. You should now and again bring back vague memories of it.'

How strange she should say this, because four times since Bob's death I've had vivid meetings with him in dreams. Twice I awoke early in the morning with such a feeling of exhilaration and with memories too precious to forget, that I had to get up at once and put them down on paper.

On looking at my records now, they seem strange, vague and jumbled — past and present confused. But the outstanding memory is that I met Bob in the flesh, and he held me in his arms. I awoke strengthened, all my loneliness gone.

I told the medium that what she had said was true and she went on:

'Your husband said to me, "When she is in her sleep state we are so often together and she should remember it." '

'It gives him great pleasure because he says that for him the parting has never taken place. He says it is so very difficult to explain because, over there, time is irrelevant. There is no night-time. There are no clocks. There is no calendar. Therefore, to them, everything is today. From his point of view you will be joining your husband *today*.

He says there are no tears in heaven since they can meet their loved ones in their sleep-state, walk with them and join in their earth-life so that you are never parted.'

The first record of a dream is headed: *Dream Night, 16th December 1971, 8 months after Bob's death*. It reads:

'For no known reason I seem to have been down to Bob's home and been talking with his sister for a long time. The house (now demolished) was gleaming with new white paint and I turned and waved at someone at the upper window as I left.

'I then made my way through the docks, of all places, where I had never been, where tremendous excavations were going on, tons of red earth being shifted, bull-dozers on every side and great pits full of water, dank, depressing and dangerous.

'My sister-in-law had left me to go for her car and I was trying to get out of the morass, when a bull-dozer driver spoke to me and told me to be careful as the earth on which I stood might give way. He showed me a way out and said that if I was interested, they ran a guided tour through the docks at 3.30 every Wednesday. I said I would make a note of the time, but couldn't promise to come, and went on my way.

'A little further on I realised that I had lost my handbag, a black lizard one, and retraced my steps to where, suddenly, a small card table had been set up, surrounded by a crowd of people. As I approached I could see my bag on the edge of the table, but at that very moment I saw a hand lift it off.

'Panic-stricken, I rushed through the red, slippery mud and pushed through the people to demand my handbag back, and there to my astonishment and wonder was Bob, half reclining, as though on a bed, surrounded by people. I noticed his dark, curly hair and thought how well he looked. And yet, in a strange way, I knew he had gone from me.

'He was wearing one of his blue shirts, without collar or tie, looking as he did when he came in very hot and ripped them off. I was not aware of what covered his feet. I was so amazed to see him, just grinning as he used to do when I had mislaid something.

'He sat up and I clasped my arms around him and burst into tears, just saying, "Oh Bob, I thought you had left me!"

'He flung his arms around me and we just rocked to and fro, his tears mingling with mine until his whole shirt-front was dark with our mingled tears. And then I said, "Now I've found you I cannot lose you again!" and dried my eyes, for I was so delighted at the comfort of his presence and we just clung to each other.

'And then the alarm — which I hadn't realised I'd set — went off. I woke up and my immediate reaction was, in the darkness, "I must tell Bob. What a funny dream!" Then — I realised — he wasn't there . . .'

My second remembered dream was two years later and my notes are headed: *Friday, June 22nd 1973 at 6 am.*

I remember coming down in the early light, feeling I *must* get down on paper my joyful meeting with Bob, in case I forgot it. I felt so happy — as happy as the birds carolling away in their dawn chorus.

This is what I wrote:

'Woke up at 5.30 am, wonderfully refreshed and so happy at meeting Bob in a dream. We were walking through a part of old London, a part of the city I did not know. Bob was talking to me.

'He was dressed in his grey Aquascutum, and walking well — as he did thirty years ago, without a stick.

'We were very happy and he kept asking me to marry him and share our future life together. I was so happy at the comfort and security of the present, and the future to look forward to. And yet, through it all, I seemed to know that he was dead and kept telling him so. This he kept denying, saying that I was mistaken and that we should be together for ever.

'I was so happy that I seemed to accept this strange, timeless position, and yet I kept thinking "What will people say when I tell them, because everyone thinks he is dead!"

'We kept walking on, admiring all the old buildings, which Bob said would all come down presently.

'He then suggested we should celebrate by going out to dinner somewhere, and called a taxi.

'We had been laughing and talking all through the evening . . . it *seemed* to be evening for that part of London appeared to be deserted.

'And then I woke up, so happy and refreshed at having spent such a long time with Bob, feeling that my whole future was secure with him; and yet . . . there was always that undercurrent . . . that he was dead.'

On these occasions the joy and Bob's nearness in our reunion would last the whole day.

Since then I've had only two other sleep-state meetings with him that I can remember. These seemed more mature — but so happy that each time I lay quivering with delight at his presence, trying to slip back into sleep again to find myself in his arms. But never could I do so.

In the first of these later dreams Bob was wearing his navy blue suit, in the second a grey suit that was my favourite. There was no sequence of events, no continued story, as in the previous dreams.

He just seemed to appear suddenly and put his arms around me . . . always a joyful reunion — but every time the wonder and ecstacy were on *my* side. A scientist friend of Bob's, interested in the occult, said this was natural, for on Bob's side there *was* no reunion. It was only on mine. And this is how it seemed. For me it was a wonderful, an amazing experience. But Bob, comforting me, was quiet and to the point, even as he always was on earth.

'But, Bob, you're alive!' I said so many times in my dream. But he kept repeating: 'I've told you so often — I'm alive and with you. Why can't you accept this?'

'I'll never doubt you again!' I remember saying, over and over again. 'Never, never!' And then, still worrying in my own mind: 'What will people say? Everyone thinks you're dead! How can I explain?'

At that point I have woken up, trying desperately to recapture that magic moment, happy and exalted.

But now I've learned that you *cannot* demand. You cannot recreate the ecstacy at will.

14 *Still seeking evidence*

All through the slowly passing years since Bob left me, I have had my so-cherished 'inspirational talks' with him and his 'guidance' — but still I have the urge to seek a sitting with a medium once or twice a year.

I get a sudden longing for a third person to tell me about him, although latterly in our 'talks' he has told me this is quite unnecessary. Many mediums have said the same thing.

'You don't really need *me*, dear,' one said to me. 'In the quiet of your home your husband can communicate with you himself.'

Of the many sittings I have had, only three or four have been unsuccessful. I really have been lucky, because the Spiritualist Association is the first to point out that no sitting can be guaranteed. So much depends on both sitter and medium — and many other factors we don't understand.

All my failures were evident from the outset, when I didn't really feel *en rapport*. Generally I am caught up, uplifted, wonderfully at peace — the strength of communication gathers momentum.

But on the occasions I speak of everything was 'heavy'.

Obviously, the medium was trying — but the lines seemed tangled. There might be a mention of Bob — then again of names that meant nothing to me. There was a feeling of strain — and after ten minutes the medium would, 'regret that it was no good.'

I always got my fee back in this event.

It can happen with men and women mediums alike.

Always disappointing, of course, but I would feel it was partly my fault — I was too worried, too anxious or restless. Certainly not in the right frame of mind.

But there was always the future to look forward to, and I have sat again with the same medium and had excellent results.

On the other hand there are certain mediums with whom I instantly felt on the same wave-length. Perhaps it is a matter of sympathetic vibrations.

Still hoping for 'voices', I had another sitting with David Young, but that strange phenomenon has never occurred again. Instead, unlike other mediums, David dwelt more on what my husband was doing on a higher plane. He began at once by saying that Bob was there — and that he had brought a dog with him.

'A small dog . . . Like a Yorkshire, yet not a Yorkshire. He's laughing about this because he wants you to know that animals do survive.'

I was pleased about this because many other mediums had spoken of Bob's being accompanied by a dog. The descriptions varied. Always a small one, sometimes described as white and furry. One medium even said she thought at first it was a large cat! No one could name the breed — not surprising because Rags was a first-cross between a King Charles Spaniel and a Maltese, a dear little perky, fluffy dog. Bob and I were always being stopped in the street by strangers asking what breed it was.

One medium called out, 'Rex! Rex!' near enough to Rags, and said he was barking in response.

Another time a medium told me Bob had *two* dogs with him.

Not possible, I told her. We'd lost only one dog.

But she insisted: 'Your husband has *two* dogs . . . one that you *both* know and one he knew as a boy . . . different breeds . . . one larger than the other.'

Of course! Bob had often told me of an Airedale he'd had and loved, long before we married.

Now David went on: 'Your husband is saying that you cannot become demanding. The more you expect, the more difficult it is for them to function.'

(Though I'd said nothing about my longing to hear the 'voices' again, I felt sure this was a small rebuke for my unspoken insistence.)

'The more you can relax and just sit waiting — for nothing in particular — the easier it is for them to produce results. He's saying that he is very busy at the moment, and that he is carrying on with many other people his research into this kind of life. He's trying to come back to earth in various ways, to show — not the trivial side of communication — but the basic reality of it, and they can and do come back to help the world.'

He then told me: 'It is not just a question of saying, "I love you, darling", and reminding you of trivial things in the past. No, many of them realise that by getting through in a scientific way, they are going to make those, who hold the destiny of the world in their hands, realise they can use their knowledge in restoring peace and giving to each person the right to live.

'This is something he and many others are trying to do. He wants you to know that he is trying to make communications through you to *other* people, of the reality of the continuity of life.

'He says that so many people doing research on this subject think of it as a form of Extra-Sensory Perception. That somehow the person, known to the medium, is picking up thoughts — if not direct from a person then in some other way — but not necessarily proving survival.

'On the other hand, what *he* is trying to prove by various channels is that he has survived death, and is very happy in doing this because he has always looked upon himself as a servant of man.

'He says that he is now part of a brotherhood looking for the truth — what we on earth would term an "intellectual outlook".

' "One must be taught," he is saying, "always to look for the simple things. Logic is all right, but it is only as good as the logic that stands up to it".'

David paused to ask: 'Does this make sense to you?'

At this stage I had to admit that I was quite lost, and said I did not understand.

'Your husband says that by being over-logical you're going to lose the point, because you're going to reach for a different sort of answer — expecting a higher and more difficult way. Whereas the way is very simple. The point he's trying to make is that *simplicity* is the key to knowledge, is the key to existence. By existing for ever, therefore, life on earth must become simple.

'The barrier of death is just the beginning. Eternity is forever. The part of eternity we live on earth is very small.

' "Don't get yourself so worried," he is saying. "Try to relax. By finding the simple way life becomes more real and there is a oneness." He wants you to know that he *has* this oneness with you — and that it is forever. Just because his earth-time body has decayed, he has not died. He lives on.'

Then David said something that brought back vividly that long-ago day of anguish:

'He's laughing about a hospital ward — and walking too much.'

Oh yes. I knew what Bob was talking about. It was after his second coronary when he was about to be discharged from hospital to come home. Always strong-willed, he insisted on walking the ward four times on crutches — strictly against orders — and slipped. Three days later he died in his sleep.

I said as much to David and added: 'And it killed him.'

'But it did *not* kill him!' David smiled. 'He says all it did was to make him alive! He's doing more now than he's ever done before — trying to show his true self, to bring his life and love towards you, to give you his own uplift, his own truth. This is *continual* and will make everything fall into place.'

Then he said: 'He's saying he still enjoys music and conversation.'

'I wish he'd have a conversation with *me*!'

'But he does!' David cut in. 'He impresses himself upon you very strongly and comes close to you. I sense this great love and joy at being always with you — and he wants you to know that this will continue.'

Two years later, on the anniversary of Bob's death, I had another sitting with David Young. This took on quite a different character. It was more like a family gathering, and of a quite personal nature. My parents came through very quickly, also friends of Bob's, and finally our little dog, Rags.

My father said he rarely appeared, but was happy to come on this occasion. David said Bob was quiet and very peaceful, and kept repeating that he wanted me to share in his peace and happiness.

Bob himself mentioned the anniversary and so did my father.

'Your husband says you know he doesn't believe in graves,' said David. 'He says, just pick a flower, one flower, and put it in a vase.'

I had already done so.

15 More communications

Bob continued always to be at hand to guide me in any domestic problem.

There was the time, for instance, when some of the elms in my garden had died and I had arranged with a family of gypsy tree-fellers to cut them down.

I knew nothing about these gypsies and must confess I rather dreaded their coming — I'd be alone in the house without a man to protect me! I waited with apprehension for the appointed day, but there was no sign of them. One, two, three days passed. No gypsies.

At last they arrived, and hotfoot on their heels up the drive strode our old friend, Harry, who had helped me so often before. All my fears fell away — just as though Bob himself had appeared. Harry immediately joined the tree-fellers and supervised the whole operation. I felt Bob had sent him.

Then there was another small panic. One evening as I switched on my bedside light I looked for my reading glasses, which normally I leave on a table beside my bed. They weren't there.

Oh well, I thought, they've probably slipped down behind the pillows, so I felt underneath them. No sign of the glasses. I stripped the bed. I drew a blank.

I ransacked the bedroom, searched my dressing-table — they *must* be in the room somewhere because I seldom took them downstairs. But the search was in vain.

Downstairs I went, looked all over the house in every possible and impossible spot. Frustrated, I climbed back upstairs, moved the bed, stripped it again!

I might just as well go to bed and forget about them till the morning — any normal person would! But no, I must find them *now*!

I took a deep breath. Calm down, I thought. And at once I felt Bob's presence, so close to me. He seemed to be saying: 'Do keep *quiet*! Go back and look on your dressing-table.'

I had already looked there — so this was absurd. But I went across the room to look again. They were there, all right. I would, of course, have found them in the morning in daylight, but they'd been almost invisible in the subdued light from the bedside lamp.

About this time I had another sitting with Ivy Northage with whom I'd sat years ago, in Bob's time, after my mother's death. This medium had been remarkable. The first thing she said was: 'Mother came in so close. You're like her. You're reminded of her every time you look in your mirror, and you say to yourself, "Mother looked exactly like that!" '

The family had often remarked on my likeness to Mother.

The medium then said: 'I don't know whether the gentleman she has with her is your husband, but there's someone in the spirit world who has that kind of affection for you, and they come together. He's taller, of course, than your mother — very gentle but has great strength in his gentleness. Not the least bit aggressive or domineering — yet he'd be able quietly to assert his authority, whether it was in dealing with business people or with you.

'There's a lovely sense of quiet efficiency . . . and he's exercising this on behalf of your affairs just now. You're travelling from one state of mind to another because you're not settled in your mind. He is piloting you and encouraging you to explore first this avenue and then another. He's not telling you what to do so much as guiding you in your own explorations.

'You will reach a satisfactory conclusion and you'll be able to handle your affairs . . . Does that make sense to you? Stop me if you don't understand.'

As my brothers and sisters had congratulated me on the way I had managed my affairs after Bob left me so suddenly, this statement was quite accurate.

Mrs Northage then told me there were several people gathered there together. 'Your husband is encouraging you to share your life and you are doing this. You're coming out of your shell, and he's encouraging you in this.'

She told me there was a definite influence from the, 'world of spirit,' helping me to rearrange my life, that they were anxious I should know of their co-operation — it wasn't a case of *my* saying, 'This is what I'm going to do, and that's the end of it.' Various aspects were involved. They had to be dealt with separately, although, 'They belonged to the same thing. He's very near to you,' she said.

I told her this made me very happy because *I* felt so close to him at times.

'I'm sure you do! He has such a gentle personality that it seems to radiate quiet confidence. It's as if as soon as he came home you'd know everything was all right.'

'That's true.'

'A lovely feeling! Try not to miss it too much, but say you have got it — on a different level. He was very much a creature of habit!'

'Oh yes!'

'There was always a certain sort of procedure when he came home — then the joy of planning your relaxation. He talks of your father and the good conversations they hold. Now he's saying: "Tell her how much I love her, how much I share in her thoughts and all her doings. I'm not in the least bit separate from her way of life and I would give a great deal if only I could say this for myself when she's feeling so sad and lonely." '

Indeed, I knew only too well I couldn't get near him if I was particularly depressed.

Mrs Northage told me then that he was saying: 'So often she calls out to me, "Why did it have to be *me*? Why did you have to leave me?" I can only echo my gratitude that it was not *I* who was left behind to await her. She's so much more capable than I about these things. I know it's hard, but it would be harder still if our positions were reversed — *I* couldn't have endured to wait on that side for her.'

The medium said I must have been sending out thoughts to him, and he was answering them, stressing how much harder it would have been for him.

'Your husband says, "I know that I can link up with your thoughts, and this is a great consolation. Try and respond . . . you know I am here and I'll support and assist you. Take this for granted! In this way all I have to give you, you're able to receive and utilise. I come with you on your various little jaunts." He talks about this as if they were little visits to people who knew him. He speaks of "Jessie" here with him.'

'That was a very old friend of his,' I said.

'He's now talking of changes. He was very much immersed in business?' she asked.

'He was devoted to it.'

'And he says there have been great changes in their policy since he passed.'

This was rather remarkable because this is exactly what had happened.

Again he spoke of his sudden passing, with no time to warn me.

'Now he speaks of the garden which he loved and says there's a replica in his world, where you visit him. He says the trees are much taller now.'

'Yes, I've had to have them lopped.'

'And he talks of a special tree being "top-heavy" lower down! Do you understand?'

'Oh yes, I do,' I told her. 'It was his favourite tree — a species of acer. It's shaped like an enormous mushroom — he always pruned the lower branches. Now I have to do it!'

'Ah! That's why he talks of it being too thick below . . . You have help in your garden, even if intermittent, and he's so pleased that it is forthcoming. I see you . . . talking to someone and explaining what you want done. It's as if he is with you. He's so anxious you should know this. The whole point of communication is to emphasise that he's with you, in your home, sharing your life with you. He comes to you and you're aware of it. He shares these experiences. It's almost as if he can repeat word for word what you said, because he was there with you.'

Mrs Northage then switched to another aspect. 'You travelled a lot in your married life. He talks about enjoying the trips, and the undiscovered places you found, before they became popular.'

'That's very true. We had wonderful holidays in Ireland.'

Again she changed the subject. 'Your weakest spot is your over-sensitivity.'

I said I was very conscious of this. 'My husband *always* said that!'

Mrs Northage smiled. 'Your husband is quite optimistic about this. He says how much more sensible you are about it! You get it off your chest and talk about it. You're very progressive and he's happy about it. He advises you. Not verbally but by influencing your train of thought. You suddenly *know* what you must do, and what you must not do.'

'I know this.'

'It's as if he feeds your mind, rather than your saying, "Give me the words and I'll listen!" They float into your mind, almost uninvited.'

This seemed to describe so accurately what actually happens, and I said I knew this was so.

'These are authentic — as opposed to deliberately trying to get phraseology . . . He's got such a happy laugh! He enjoys things just as he used to. He has no inhibitions. If he was happy and pleased, he showed it. If he didn't enjoy himself, he just didn't stay.'

'True!'

She said his personality was quite remarkable. Then: 'He had a lovely speaking voice, and he enjoyed singing and music, didn't he?'

'Yes. He had a beautiful tenor voice.'

'In a symbolic sense, he's placing a beautiful cloak

around you . . . and I feel he has this power to protect you, to keep you warm, to keep you safe in this cloak of his love, wherever you go.

'You're never separate from him. And I feel he wants you to know that wherever you go that cloak is for ever around you . . . "Give her my assurance," he says, "that nothing can harm her because my love is around her." '

She broke off. Then suddenly: 'A watch needs attention! Here's another of his little idiosyncrasies! He couldn't bear anything to be wrong with clocks!'

'Yes, he adored clocks, collected them and adjusted them every weekend.'

Mrs Northage smiled. 'He was very precise. "I don't want them slow, and I don't want them fast, I want them *right*!" '

Her information was so accurate it amazed me. I laughed. I told her he aimed to have every clock in the house chime at the same moment.

'I still have his notebook,' I said, 'marked "Calibrations". In it he used to enter the variations and adjustments each week.'

Then I mentioned the incident with the psychic clocksmith who had felt Bob's presence in the house.

'I don't know when I have been so aware of his nearness,' the medium said. 'This closeness is one you share in your own home. He's not just using me. It's what goes on all the time. It's so easy for me to tell you what you're thinking, and what you were doing, because he's there and this is what he wants to get over to you. You're not alone.

'I think they do remarkably well in their efforts to reach us. He's much more concerned in assuring you of his presence with you *at home* than coming through me here. This doesn't bother him at all. He's merely giving you the corroboration you've asked for. He wants you to go away with the positive thought that he's beside you, walking with you, driving with you, staying at home with you . . .'

As I had once said in one of our 'inspirational talks', I now repeated:

'I've often wondered how he can be in two places at once.'

'It isn't like that there, dear,' Mrs Northage replied. 'It is a mental world. The nearest you can get to it is a dream experience. You know how you can be in all sorts of places in a dream, and you take it as a matter of course. I think it's rather like that. He's instantaneously with you in thought.

'Remember that love is the abiding factor. Where love is, *he* is but this does not confine him to your house or garden. It's a kind of perspective which includes your home and his own spiritual sphere as well. It's very hard to understand from a physical perspective. He's very definitely here.'

She then made a statement I thought odd: 'You have definite connections with masonic symbols!'

I said neither Bob nor my father had been masons, but she insisted there *were* masonic symbols. 'You cannot deny it!'

I then remembered that a cousin who had been very close to me *was* a mason, and said so. This seemed to satisfy her.

'They're quite unmistakable and they have a very powerful occult influence. I think what your husband is trying to convey to me is that they have a deeper significance than we realise on the earth plane.'

Finally the medium said: 'When I come near the end I try to tie up the "scraps" I haven't given you . . . There is someone who worked for you called Gladys. She has passed on.'

I remembered her. Other mediums had mentioned her name before.

'Bob used to call her "his coalman",' I said, 'because she could carry two buckets of coal at one time!'

'Yes. He's laughing about this too. He says, "Just remind her of Gladys." Obviously he has seen her. But it's quite clear from him that she worked for you.

'He's wonderfully clear, dear, quite remarkable. No hesitation . . . So often one is ambiguous. But not your husband.'

113

I mentioned that I had not sat with her for many years, yet I longed for someone to confirm my feeling.

'Yes. You feel it could so easily be wishful thinking — but this is what he wants you to realise: He's always with you. In a way, he says, it's not necessary for you to have sittings. He can communicate with you himself.'

And so I felt satisfied.

16   Still more words

Another autumn was here again, filling the air with the pungent smell of wood-smoke from bonfires, scattering its gold coinage over the countryside, bringing with it a longing to have further tangible evidence of Bob's survival, from a third person.

I got in touch with the Spiritualist Association and made an appointment with a medium, Gladys Fieldhouse. I chose her name at random. I had never met her. But from the moment we met I felt an immediate happy affinity.

'I feel here,' she said, 'a gentleman with a great deal of strength, even more mental than physical, a well-built man and yet — as gentle as a kitten.'

There was a slight pause, and then she laughed.

'What on earth is he talking about? He says, "Are you still making your hats?" It's funny, but he seems delighted with your lovely hats. He always liked to see you in new things and with beautiful things around you.'

This amused me and I told her he'd often mentioned my hats before. He was always interested, particularly as I made them myself.

'He was always sincere and outspoken,' she said, 'if he didn't agree with anything. There was no nonsense about him.'

'I'm going to your home,' she said. 'A lovely garden, so natural looking, and into your house. It's full of such lovely pieces, each with a memory. It's not just a house, but a home — warm, lovely, and it speaks of love. Your husband says if he walks about it he can touch his personal belongings. Do you still have any personal things of his?'

I told her of the dressing-gown still hanging in the bath-room and the old gardening jacket in the kitchen.

'He has certainly never left you — no shadow of doubt. I feel you're very aware of him. After his passing you set out on a quest, as it were, and you've found it satisfying.

'I feel that both of you knew of spiritualism before his passing, but it was because of his passing that you decided to investigate. You've done this with an open but very sympathetic mind and have had quite amazing evidence and results.'

'Quite true.'

'Not only have you had evidence from your husband and *about* your husband, but you have also met other loved ones. This has surprised you, because you've not been thinking of them.'

I agreed.

Now Mrs Fieldhouse seemed slightly puzzled.

'I don't quite understand what I'm getting now. It's something about — writing. But it's not notes or letters. I feel you have written an article — or a paper or magazine. As if, as it were, you wished to spread the good news of your husband's survival.'

This seemed to me astonishing evidence. I told her I'd written two articles for magazines on this subject.

'But there is also something else going on.' She still seemed puzzled. 'I don't know why I'm saying this — but why does your husband refer to a book?'

I gave an affirmative nod.

'Well, he seems to know all about this. But I'm a little in the dark! Was it a book he wanted you to write?'

'Yes,' I answered. 'Soon after his death he kept mention-ing it in his "inspirational talks". He even told me to buy a tape-recorder to make things easier.'

Mrs Fieldhouse smiled. 'And you're writing it, and it will be successful and people will read it. I feel you're still gathering evidence for this book. But you have approached this with a scientific mind because you want it to be *absolutely* truthful. I feel both you and your husband are truthful people.

116

'Although you have an understanding of the spirit world and the mechanics of mediumship, you feel you want the truth. You don't expect miracles, and I feel your husband has worked jolly hard to get through and give you the evidence. He'll continue to give you this in various ways. He says it's not always possible to communicate as he would like because he can only shape the pot according to the clay in his hands.'

She said then that she did not know whether he was the, 'Kind of person to use metaphors,' but that he didn't want me to be disappointed if all I was seeking didn't turn up.

'I don't think,' she explained, 'he's referring to this sitting, but to *all* your investigations. Where does the scientific part of things come in? I feel you have lived with a scientist.'

I told her I had indeed.

'I'm a little confused . . . I feel you have submitted evidence for people to test. Some have agreed, others said they were not sure. I feel you certainly have enough material for your book, and you're well in the way of putting it together — tying up loose ends. But you're still wanting the final chapters, yet you will find it is difinitely "following on" . . . the more you look back on what you've written . . . it is truly remarkable.'

I found it remarkable that she had 'diagnosed' the situation so accurately when she could not possibly have known anything about me or my activities.

'Wait a minute!' she said suddenly. 'Before your husband passed into spirit, did he lose his voice, or find difficulty in speaking?'

I was bewildered. I said, 'No.'

'I'm getting a little confusion here. I feel strongly from your husband there was heart trouble and a quick passing. There was no time to make any arrangements.'

That was certainly true, I said.

'Then why does he whisper to you? Why? If he didn't lose his voice? I'm not sure what I'm getting! I feel he has tried at some time to speak to you . . . Have you heard his voice very softly? I feel I want to whisper to you. I want to say, "Darling!" Do you understand? I feel sure you must have heard this. It all seems a little odd and I can't change it. You must have heard it!'

By now I realised how brilliant this medium was — trying to tell me of Bob's whisper appearing on tape, 'I love you, darling.' She knew nothing of this extraordinary event either.

Suddenly she switched to another subject.

'Have you known people in the theatre?'

I said I had.

'I feel you had a full and wonderful life right up to your husband's passing and, although you enjoyed each other's company, there were moments when you loved to have people around you. The house would be full of laughter. But you greatly enjoyed the peace when they all went away!

'Your husband was a keen student of nature and people. He was always extremely polite and kind, but he could weigh people up and was never wrong. And you had that wonderful way of looking at each other. Words weren't needed — thoughts were conveyed from one to the other.'

This made me smile for so often Bob had said: 'All right! You needn't bother to say anything. I can see from your face!'

'You were both so full of life,' she went on. 'The thought of death, of parting, never occurred to you. You were both deep thinkers. You discussed many things together and had this wonderful understanding. You have a photograph of him at home . . . in a prominent position, with flowers beside it.'

'Yes,' I said.

'You are well aware of his presence and feel his eyes are watching you. In spirit he is very close. Now, have you any questions, please?'

There was one question to which I very much wanted the answer.

'Can you see my husband?'

'No. I *sense* him, more than see him. When I say a well-built gentleman, I don't feel it's so much his *size*, as his

118

character and strength — that aura around him you are so aware of . . . The same kind of thing you spoke of when I first entered the room . . . It came from your husband to you — and it's coming from him now! It's as though he's oblivious of *me*. Just looking at you, standing in front of you, giving out this aura of peace and tranquillity.'

In the last few years I have sat with many other mediums who all seem to agree on the salient points. They insist Bob is very near me, both in the house and garden — wherever I go. They all talk of his sudden passing, the shock to both of us, his happiness in working in his present surroundings — though this will not be complete until I join him — his providing a 'pipe-line' of friends to help me in my loneliness. And this is all so true, because since his death friends seem to turn up to comfort me.

He tells me that when I drive he 'puts his hands over mine' to shield me from accidents, that I can always reach him, even in my sleep.

Two years later I sat with Gladys Fieldhouse again. During this most satisfying sitting, she said:

'Your husband is keeping a promise that he made in his life, to love and cherish you and I feel that with him — as with all people where there is great love — it isn't in fact *until* death do us part', it is even *after* death. And this great love is coming to you now.'

Then the medium came back to that other subject she had mentioned at the previous sitting:

'I feel there is great interest taken in some work you have done. Do you understand this?'

I said I was pretty sure I did.

'It seems to me this particular job is completed in some way and you're feeling quite pleased about things yourself?'

I hesitated.

'You seem a little hesitant! Perhaps it hasn't turned out exactly as you would wish? But I feel that a lot of effort went into this, and that spirit — your husband in particular — is pleased because you're reaching through to people in some way or other, to make them sit up and listen.'

She went on: 'But, as one task is finished, so I feel in your mind there are plans for another. In spirit the blueprints are being laid, and there is more work for you to do. They are prompting you in that direction, and one thing leads to another. Questions are asked and answers given — and all the time I get a great prompting from the spirit . . . I want to say, take up the pen again! Does that make sense?'

Her assessment of events left me dumbfounded. I waited for her to say more.

'I don't know!' She seemed to hesitate. 'I — get the pen. But — do you type yourself?'

I said I did.

'Because I've got a typewriter also! They may be referring to the pen, but meaning the typewriter! I feel this has helped to fill a big gap in your life — and to give you an incentive to go forward.'

I always compose on the typewriter. Mrs Fieldhouse had no idea I'd been a journalist.

Now she said: 'Your mind is alert and this is why the spirit world has decided to use you. So, will you take their love — and particularly the love of your husband — and know that there is a purpose and a plan in your living? You've made up your mind to carry out this plan, as far as you are able, and spirit will help you to complete it.'

I asked her then: 'Does Bob still communicate with me?'

'I feel he's never ceased to try and communicate. But he found it extremely difficult to do this, in the way you would like and he would like, because he's trying to bring this about in a more physical way. *That* is extremely difficult. I feel . . . he is trying to achieve something that even guides and teachers cannot achieve!'

I told her this was typical of Bob's attitude on earth — to try and achieve perfection.

Finally Mrs Fieldhouse said: 'I feel you loved each other deeply, but this little separation will make it stronger. The experience of being apart will make the coming together much more wonderful. I know — beyond a shadow of doubt — he links to you each evening when you talk to him and say "Goodnight!" He is *there* and greets you with a kiss because, during sleep state, you are always together.'

17   Lasting comfort

The last sitting I have had was with Mrs Ivy Scott from whom I had had such satisfying results in the past.

'You have a mediumistic quality of your own,' she began. 'Otherwise, however good a medium may be, the voices would not be so clear. You emanate a certain amount of force yourself.'

As others had done so often before, she stressed Bob's nearness — especially at night, or when I am quiet and alone. She then described the chair he always sat in, next to my own by the fire.

In a figurative way she spoke of the 'cloak' thrown around me and the house, to protect me from harm. As I've already mentioned in previous chapters, other mediums have likened this to a gold or blue net.

Then Mrs Scott spoke again of 'a book': 'Your husband has put a pen in your hand. 'And he says, "Write! She is quite capable!" And you do write. The spirit people are very close to you, sharpening your memory, and your husband is encouraging you very much.'

Mrs Scott can have had no idea that the book was almost ready to deliver to the publishers.

I still have evidence of Bob's practical help in my daily life, in all sorts of — sometimes — trivial ways. Yet the 'messages' are always to the point and save me endless bother.

There was the time I mislaid the key to the filing cabinet. (Keys seem to be my downfall!) I needed it urgently to find some important papers.

I searched everywhere, in all the most likely places, but

drew a blank. Then, clear as a bell, the thought came into my head: 'Look in the tureen on the dresser!'

There have always been three or four spare bunches of keys in that receptacle since Bob's time. There were stacks of them, all shapes and sizes. Did I have to go through the lot? It was quite unlikely the one I wanted would be among them. However! The message *would* persist. I'd have no peace until I responded.

The first key I picked up was no good . . . the second fitted perfectly!

I had further strange proof of Bob's presence about the house — a presence I've now become so accustomed to.

Someone comes to the house regularly to deliver paraffin. I call her my 'paraffin lady'. One day when she had come I happened to mention I had lost my husband.

Her response was astonishing. 'You amaze me!' she said. 'I'd no idea you were a widow. When you took me into your husband's study the other day I thought he was in the next room. All the time I've been calling I always thought he was about somewhere. It must be the way you speak of him!'

That Christmas I went to a Spiritualist Healer. She had never mentioned Bob before, but this time when I thanked her, I said.

'I feel as though someone had put their arms around me.'

'That's your husband,' she answered quietly. 'I felt him come into the room with you — and he's still here. He wants me to give you a message: Will you *please*, he says, buy yourself an expensive Christmas present!'

Later she rang me to ask if she had made her meaning clear, 'because he's so insistent!' she said.

I was able to tell her that only that morning I'd looked at the empty bottle of expensive French perfume that Bob had always bought me for Christmas and reflected sadly that I'd never have another one.

'*Please* treat yourself,' she urged. 'It's obviously what he wants you to do.'

The next morning I did just that.

Epilogue

And now, after nine years, my book is being published, and yet I cannot write FINIS across the page, for each day makes me aware of Bob's presence, often in the most trifling way.

Even as I revised the final draft last week I felt he still had a finger in the pie!

I have already written about David Ellis, who had investigated the Raudive Voices. It was midnight and I felt the urge to get in touch with him to ask if he would recheck his contribution to this book.

He lives a good distance away from me, but I felt desperate for his help, and considered telephoning him. But at midnight? That seemed ridiculous! So I packed up the manuscript ready to post to the publishers next morning and went to bed.

I am a late riser and at ten o'clock the next morning, just as I had made a cup of tea, there was a ring at the front doorbell.

I went to open the door, and found — David Ellis! I was staggered.

I had not seen him for eighteen months.

'I was passing your way,' he said, 'and wondered whether I dared call!'

I said: 'You couldn't have arrived at a more opportune moment!'

I gave him a cup of tea, undid the parcel of manuscript and left him with it so that he could, if necessary, bring it up to date from his angle — it was several years previously that I had written about the incidents concerning him.

Now I felt happy that the scientist who had been interested in my 'voice' on tape had been able to check the accuracy of my account.

Nothing that I have written can be proved. All the events in themselves may seem to some to be small and trivial — just straws in the wind, but they all blow in the same direction and form a pattern. You can see straws, but not the wind that blows them. You only feel its influence. Is it the unseen strength of Bob's love that has produced this pattern of my life? I think it is.

The dreadful finality of separation by death has vanished. I believe that Bob is with me all the way, trying by various means to assure me that this is no end, that when I finally cross the bridge he will fling wide his arms, with his old welcoming smile, to greet me as he always did after a long separation.

Then, our spirits entwined for ever, together we shall climb upwards towards God, the Almighty Father, the Logos, the Truth, now incomprehensible to our finite minds.

'For now we see through a glass darkly; but then face to face, now I know in part; but then I shall know even as also I am known.

And now abideth faith, hope, love, these three; but the greatest of these is love.'

The end

LIFE AFTER LIFE

by RAYMOND A. MOODY JR. M.D.

A man is dying and, as he reaches the point of greatest physical distress, he hears himself pronounced dead by his doctor. He begins to hear an uncomfortable noise, a loud ringing or buzzing, and at the same time feels himself moving very rapidly through a long, dark tunnel. After this, he finds himself outside of his own physical body . . . Soon, other things begin to happen. Others come to meet and help him. He glimpses the spirits of relatives and friends who have already died, and a loving, warm spirit of a kind he has never encountered before — *a being of light* — appears before him.

Over the past five years, Dr Raymond Moody has studied more than one hundred subjects who have experienced 'clinical death' and been revived. Their accounts of this experience are startlingly similar in detail.

'It is research like Dr Moody presents in his book that will enlighten many and will confirm what we have been taught for two thousand years — that there is life after death.'
— From the foreword by Elisabeth Kubler-Ross, M.D.

0 552 14609 2 £1.00

ALSO AVAILABLE BY THE SAME AUTHOR:

REFLECTIONS ON LIFE AFTER LIFE

Further investigation of an extraordinary phenomenon — survival of life after bodily death.

0 552 11140 X £1.00

GHOSTS OF WALES

by PETER UNDERWOOD

Wales has many ghosts and amid the beauty of its vales and hills, its towns and villages and hamlets, there are literally hundreds of haunted spots. Peter Underwood, the eminent psychical researcher and well-known broadcaster, travels through the country, walking where shadowy phantom figures have walked, talking where ghostly voices have talked, driving where ghost coach-and-horses have driven and pausing where ghosts have paused before him. From Aberaeron in Dyfed to Welshpool in Powis, and many stops along the way, the reader is introduced to a region whose folklore and daily life is more visited by the occult than anywhere else in the British Isles.

0 552 11315 8 £1.25

A SELECTED LIST OF FINE NOVELS
THAT APPEAR IN CORGI

While every effort is made to keep prices low, it is sometimes necessary to increase prices at short notice. Corgi Books reserve the right to show new retail prices on covers which may differ from those previously advertised in the text or elsewhere.

The prices shown below were correct at the time of going to press. (Nov. '81)

☐ 11567 3	THE PROPHECIES OF NOSTRADAMUS	Erika Cheetham	£1.75
☐ 08800 5	CHARIOTS OF THE GODS?	Erich Von Daniken	£1.35
☐ 09083 2	RETURN TO THE STARS	Erich Von Daniken	95p
☐ 09689 X	THE GOLD OF THE GODS	Erich Von Daniken	£1.25
☐ 10073 0	IN SEARCH OF ANCIENT GODS	Erich Von Daniken	85p
☐ 10371 3	MIRACLES OF THE GODS	Erich Von Daniken	£1.50
☐ 10870 7	ACCORDING TO THE EVIDENCE	Erich Von Daniken	£1.25
☐ 11591 6	THE AIRMEN WHO WOULD NOT DIE	John G. Fuller	£1.50
☐ 11020 5	THE GHOST OF FLIGHT 401	John G. Fuller	£1.50
☐ 11220 8	MY SEARCH FOR THE GHOST OF FLIGHT 401	Elizabeth Fuller	£1.00
☐ 09430 7	THE U.F.O. EXPERIENCE — A SCIENTIFIC INQUIRY	J. Allen Hynek	95p
☐ 10928 2	THE ANCIENT MAGIC OF THE PYRAMIDS	Ken Johnson	80p
☐ 14609 2	LIFE AFTER LIFE	Raymond A. Moody Jr. M.D.	£1.00
☐ 11140 X	REFLECTIONS ON LIFE AFTER LIFE	Raymond A. Moody Jr. M.D.	£1.00
☐ 10707 7	THREE LIVES	T. Lobsang Rampa	75p
☐ 10628 3	DOCTOR FROM LHASA	T. Lobsang Rampa	£1.25
☐ 11464 2	THE CAVE OF THE ANCIENTS	T. Lobsang Rampa	£1.50
☐ 10416 7	I BELIEVE	T. Lobsang Rampa	£1.25
☐ 10189 3	THE SAFFRON ROBE	T. Lobsang Rampa	£1.25
☐ 10087 0	AS IT WAS!	T. Lobsang Rampa	£1.00
☐ 09834 5	THE THIRD EYE	T. Lobsang Rampa	£1.25
☐ 11413 8	THE RAMPA STORY	T. Lobsang Rampa	95p
☐ 11283 6	AUTUMN LADY	Mama San Ra-Ab Rampa	85p
☐ 11315 8	GHOSTS OF WALES	Peter Underwood	£1.25

ORDER FORM

All these books are available at your book shop or newsagent, or can be ordered direct from the publisher. Just tick the titles you want and fill in the form below.

CORGI BOOKS, Cash Sales Department, P.O. Box 11, Falmouth, Cornwall.

Please send cheque or postal order, no currency.

Please allow cost of book(s) plus the following for postage and packing:

U.K. Customers—Allow 40p for the first book, 18p for the second book and 13p for each additional book ordered, to a maximum charge of £1.49.

B.F.P.O. and Eire—Allow 40p for the first book, 18p for the second book plus 13p per copy for the next 3 books, thereafter 7p per book.

Overseas Customers—Allow 60p for the first book and 18p per copy for each additional book.

NAME (block letters) ....

ADDRESS ....

(Nov. '81) ....